**Cultural And
Geographical
Exploration**

Jerusalem and the Holy Land

CHRONICLES FROM *NATIONAL GEOGRAPHIC*

Cultural And Geographical Exploration

Cultural And Geographical Exploration

Jerusalem and the Holy Land

CHRONICLES FROM *NATIONAL GEOGRAPHIC*

Arthur M. Schlesinger, jr.
Senior Consulting Editor

Fred L. Israel
General Editor

CHELSEA HOUSE PUBLISHERS

Philadelphia

CHELSEA HOUSE PUBLISHERS

Editor in Chief Stephen Reginald
Managing Editor James D. Gallagher
Production Manager Pamela Loos
Art Director Sara Davis
Director of Photography Judy L. Hasday
Senior Production Editor Lisa Chippendale

First Printing

1 3 5 7 9 8 6 4 2

Library of Congress Cataloging-in-Publication Data

Jerusalem and the Holy Land: chronicles from National Geographic.
    p. cm.—(Cultural and geographical explorations)
    Summary: Articles from National Geographic present an account of
    Muslim village life, the travel impressions of a British historian,
    and a description of the Passover celebration of a small group of
    Orthodox Jews known as Samaritans.
    ISBN 0-7910-5101-3
    1. Palestine—Social life and customs—Juvenile literature.
    2. Palestinian Arabs—Israel—Social life and customs—Juvenile
    literature. 3. Passover (Samaritan)—Juvenile literature.
    [1. Palestine—Social life and customs.   2. Palestinian Arabs—
    Israel. 3. Passover (Samaritan)] I. Series.
    DS112.J47   1999
    915.694—dc21   98-44248
                                    CIP
                                    AC

CONTENTS

"THE GREATEST EDUCATIONAL JOURNAL"

When the first *National Geographic* magazine appeared in October 1888, the United States totaled 38 states. Grover Cleveland was President. The nation's population hovered around 60 million. Great Britain's Queen Victoria also ruled as the Empress of India. William II became Kaiser of Germany that year. Tsar Alexander III ruled Russia and the Turkish Empire stretched from the Balkans to the tip of Arabia. To Westerners, the Far East was still a remote and mysterious land. Throughout the world, riding the back of an animal was the principle means of transportation. Unexplored and unmarked places dotted the global map.

On January 13, 1888, thirty-three men—scientists, cartographers, inventors, scholars, and explorers—met in Washington, D. C. They had accepted an invitation from Gardiner Greene Hubbard (1822-1897), the first president of the Bell Telephone Co. and a leader in the education of the deaf, to form the National Geographic Society "to increase and diffuse geographic knowledge." One of the assembled group noted that they were the "first explorers of the Grand Canyon and the Yellowstone, those who had carried the American flag farthest north, who had measured the altitude of our famous mountains, traced the windings of our coasts and rivers, determined the distribution of flora and fauna, enlightened us in the customs of the aborigines, and marked out the path of storm and flood." Nine months later, the first issue of *National Geographic* magazine was sent out to 165 charter members. Today, more than a century later, membership has grown to an astounding 11 million in more than 170 nations. Several times that number regularly read the monthly issues of the *National Geographic* magazine.

The first years were difficult ones for the new magazine. The earliest volumes seem dreadfully scientific and quite dull. The articles in Volume I, No. 1 set the tone—W. M Davis, "Geographic Methods in Geologic Investigation," followed by W. J. McGee, "The Classification of Geographic Forms by Genesis." Issues came out erratically—three in 1889, five in 1890, four in 1891; and two in 1895. In January 1896 "an illustrated monthly" was added to the title. The November issue that year contained a photograph of a half-naked Zulu bride and bridegroom in their wedding finery staring full face into the camera. But, a reader must have wondered what to make of the accompanying text: "These people . . . possess some excellent traits, but are horribly cruel when once they have smelled blood." In hopes of expanding circulation, the Board of Managers offered newsstand copies at $.25 each and began to accept advertising. But the magazine essentially remained unchanged. Circulation only rose slightly.

In January 1898, shortly after Gardiner Greene Hubbard's death, his son-in-law Alexander Graham Bell (1847-1922) agreed to succeed him as the second president of the National Geographic Society. Bell invented the telephone in 1876 and, while pursuing his life long goal of improving the lot of the deaf, had turned his amazingly versatile mind to contemplating such varied problems as human flight, air conditioning, and popularizing geography. The society then had about 1100 members—the magazine was on the edge of bankruptcy. Bell did not want the job. He wrote in his diary though that he accepted leadership of the Society "in order to save it. Geography is a fascinating subject and it can be made interesting," he told the board of directors. Bell abandoned the unsuccessful attempt to increase circulation through newsstand sales. "Our journal," he wrote "should go to members, people who believe in our work and want to help." He understood that the lure for prospective members should be an association with a society that made it possible for the average person to share with kings and scientists the excitement of sending an expedition to a strange land or an explorer to an inaccessible region. This idea, more than any other, has been responsible for the growth of the National Geographic Society and for the popularity of the magazine. "I can well remember," recalled Bell in 1912, "how the idea was laughed at that we should ever reach a membership of ten thousand." That year it had soared to 107,000!

Bell attributed this phenomenal growth though to one man who had transformed the *National Geographic* magazine into "the greatest educational journal in the world"—Gilbert H. Grosvenor (1875-1966). Bell had hired the then 24-year-old Grosvenor in 1899 as the Society's first full-time employee "to put some life into the magazine." He personally escorted the new editor, who will become his son-in-law, to the Society's headquarters—a small rented room shared with the American Forestry Association on the fifth floor of a building, long since gone, across 15th street from the U. S. Treasury in downtown Washington. Grosvenor remembered the headquarters "littered with old magazines, newspapers, and a few record books and six enormous boxes crammed with *Geographics* returned by the newsstands." "No desk!" exclaimed Bell. "I'll send you mine." That afternoon, delivery men brought Grosvenor a large walnut rolltop and the new editor began to implement Bell's instructions—to transform the magazine from one of cold geographic fact "expressed in hieroglyphic terms which the layman could not understand into a vehicle for carrying the living, breathing, human-interest truth about this great world of ours to the people." And what did Bell consider appropriate "geographic subjects?" He replied: "The world and all that is in it is our theme."

Grosvenor shared Bell's vision of a great society and magazine which would disseminate geographic knowledge. "I thought of geography in terms of its Greek root: *geographia*—a description of the world," he later wrote. "It thus becomes the most catholic of subjects, universal in appeal, and embracing nations, people, plants, birds, fish. We would never lack interesting subjects." To attract readers, Grosvenor had to change the public attitude toward geography which he knew was regarded as "one of the dullest of all subjects, something to inflict upon schoolboys and avoid in later life." He wondered why certain books which relied heavily on geographic description remained popular—Charles Darwin's *Voyage of the Beagle*, Richard Dana, Jr.'s *Two Years Before the Mast* and even Herodotus' *History*. Why did readers for generations, and with Herodotus' travels, for twenty centuries return to these books? What did these volumes, which used so many geographic descriptions, have in common? What was the secret? According to Grosvenor, the answer was that "each was an accurate, eyewitness, firsthand account. Each contained simple straightforward writing—writing that sought to make pictures in the reader's mind."

Gilbert Grosvenor was editor of the *National Geographic* magazine for 55 years, from 1899 until 1954. Each of the 660 issues under his direction had been a highly readable geography textbook. He took Bell's vision and made it a reality. Acclaimed as "Mr. Geography," he discovered the earth anew for himself and for millions around the globe. He charted the dynamic course which the National Geographic Society and its magazine followed for more than half a century. In so doing, he forged an instrument for world education and understanding unique in this or any age. Under his direction, the *National Geographic* magazine grew from a few hundred copies—he recalled carrying them to the post office on his back—to more than five million at the time of his retirement as editor, enough for a stack 25 miles high.

This Chelsea House series celebrates Grosvenor's first twenty-five years as editor of the *National Geographic*. "The mind must see before it can believe," said Grosvenor. From the earliest days, he filled the magazine with photographs and established another Geographic principle—to portray people in their natural attire or lack of it. Within his own editorial committee, young Grosvenor encountered the prejudice that photographs had to be "scientific." Too often, this meant dullness. To Grosvenor, every picture and sentence had to be interesting to the layman. "How could you educate and inform if you lost your audience by boring your readers?" Grosvenor would ask his staff. He persisted and succeeded in making the *National Geographic* magazine reflect this fascinating world.

To the young-in-heart of every age there is magic in the name *National Geographic*. The very words conjure up enchanting images of faraway places, explorers and scientists, sparkling seas and dazzling mountain peaks, strange plants, animals, people, and customs. The small society founded in 1888 "for the increase and diffusion of geographic knowledge" grew, under the guidance of one man, to become a great force for knowledge and understanding. This achievement lies in the genius of Gilbert H. Grosvenor, the architect and master builder of the National Geographic Society and its magazine.

Fred L. Israel
The City College of the City University of New York

JERUSALEM AND THE HOLY LAND: AN OVERVIEW

FRED L. ISRAEL

Jerusalem and the Holy Land, 1914–1920 contains an account of Muslim village life; the travel impressions of noted British historian James Bryce; and a remarkable description of a blood sacrifice in celebration of Passover by the Samaritans, a small group of Orthodox Jews who trace their ancestry to the Biblical tribe of Levi. Many photographs are included.

Today, Israel comprises most of the Biblical Holy Land. According to the Bible, Abraham, the Father of the Jewish people, established a Semitic population in this region between 1800 and 1500 B.C. Two great religions—Judaism and Christianity—originated here. Muslims, the followers of the Islamic religion, also consider the Holy Land a sacred place.

During the 8th century B.C., the Assyrians, a people who lived in what is now Iraq, conquered the ancient Israelites. Subsequently, the Persians, Romans, and Muslim Arabs occupied the area. Muslim power controlled the region until the early 1900s. Most rulers allowed Christians and Jews to keep their religion. However, a good deal of the population gradually accepted Islam and the Arab-Islamic culture.

Around 1000 A.D., the Seljuks, a Turkish people, dominated Palestine. (In the second century A.D., the Romans had named the area Palaestina, which became Palestine in English.) The Seljuks gained control of Jerusalem in 1071. Christian crusaders from Europe now began an armed effort to retake the land where their religion had begun. In 1099, they captured Jerusalem and held the city until 1187 when the Muslim leader Saladin successfully attacked Palestine. In the 16th century, Palestine became part of the Ottoman Empire.

Beginning in the 1500s, Jews from European nations, especially those bordering the Mediterranean Sea, began to migrate to Palestine. In the late 1800s, the oppression of Jews in Eastern Europe set off a large movement of Jewish refugees to the Holy Land. Some Jews formed a movement called Zionism which sought to make Palestine an independent Jewish nation. At the same time, Palestine's Arab population grew rapidly. It is estimated that the total population of Palestine in 1914 stood at about 725,000—615,000 people were Arabs and 85,000 were Jews. Jerusalem's population that year was nearly 75,000—48,000 Jews, 10,000 Muslims, and about 17,000 Christians.

During World War I (1914–1918) the Ottoman Empire joined Germany and Austria-Hungary against the Allied powers. An Ottoman military government ruled Palestine. Great Britain offered to support Arab demands for post-war independence from the Ottomans in return for Arab support for the Allied cause. Beginning in 1916, many Arabs began to revolt against Ottoman rule in the belief that Britain would establish independent Arab nations throughout the Middle East. The Arabs maintained that Palestine was included in the area promised to them. The British denied this claim. Likewise, in an attempt to gain Jewish support for its war effort, the British issued the Balfour Declaration in 1917. This document stated Britain's support for the creation of a Jewish national homeland in Palestine that would not violate the civil and religious rights of non-Jewish people. At the end of the war, the League of Nations gave Great Britain a provisional mandate to administer Palestine (1920).

The three articles in this volume describe Jerusalem and the Holy Land at the start of the First World War (1914); at the defeat of the Ottomans (1917); and at the establishment of the British mandate (1920).

VILLAGE LIFE IN THE HOLY LAND

By John D. Whiting

A description of the life of the present-day inhabitants of Palestine, showing how, in many cases, their customs are the same as in Bible times. Illustrated by photographs by the American Colony Photographers, Jerusalem.

PALESTINE, often called the Holy Land, is in a general way familiar to all of us from our study of the Bible. Few, however, realize that the manners and customs which prevailed there in Biblical days are still unchanged, even after an interval of 3,000 years. The land today is inhabited by three distinct classes: the *Bedouin*, or nomads, a wandering, war-loving race; the *Fellaheen*, who are the agriculturists, shepherds, and village dwellers, and the *Madaniyeh*, who live in the towns and cities and are artisans.

With the advent of civilization the townspeople are fast losing their ancient customs and quaint costumes, but the villagers adhere to both far more tenaciously. Still, no one knowing the country can fail to see that a time is not far distant when many of their interesting and long-lived habits of life will be things of the past.

THE VILLAGE HOME

The present-day villages are located, as a rule, either on the tops of hills, originally for protection, or near some spring or source of water. Many are built upon the foundations of dwellings whose origin dates back thousands of years. There does not exist a single example of a peasant village that has been founded in modern times.

With almost every village or district there are, to a greater or lesser extent, variations in the dialect of the Arabic they speak, their style of dress, and the homes they live in.

On the Plain of Sharon, where stone is rare or non-existent, the houses are made of sun-dried brick, the roofs thatched and covered with clay to shed the rain, while in the mountains they are built of stone, since of that material there is an inexhaustible supply.

Many have pictured in their minds Mary and Joseph, after arriving at the "inn" at Bethlehem and finding no room, being forced to turn into some barn built of timber, with lofty roof, hay mows, wooden mangers, and stalls for cattle and sheep. Such a stable has been the subject of many medieval and modern artists, but it does not present a really true picture. Let us consider the old-style village home that is most common in the districts around Jerusalem and Bethlehem, for that will give us a better idea of what happened on that first Christmas day.

The village streets are crooked, narrow, and unpaved. As in many of the countries of the Orient, farmers live close together for protection, and not on their lands: therefore in the villages there are no open fields or gardens, but house is next to house, except for the small walled-in inclosures or sheepfolds through which one generally passes when going into the dwelling.

The house itself consists of one large room, usually square. The walls, from 3 to 4 feet thick, are built of blocks of stone roughly dressed and laid in mortar, roofed over with a dome, also of stone. The outside of this roof is covered with a coating of mortar made of clay, which, on being pressed with a small stone roller or pounded with a board, becomes hard and compact enough to shed the rain (see page 3).

A steep outside staircase, unprotected by any railing, is built up to the roof, for the surface must be repaired at times. The flat, open space of the roof also forms a handy place on which to dry figs and raisins, and during the hot weather the family may sleep there at night.

THE UPPER ROOM OF THE HOUSE

Entering the door, we find that about two-thirds of the space is devoted to a raised masonry platform, some 8 to 10 feet above the ground and supported by low-domed arches. This raised space, called *el mastaby*, is the part occupied by the family, while the lower part is used for the cattle and flocks (see page 49). A few narrow stone steps lead up to the *mastaby*, and a couple of small windows pierce the wall, high up from the ground. These, as a rule, are the only means of admitting light and furnishing ventilation to the entire house. Until about half a century ago it was thought unsafe to build even medium-sized windows, and any man presuming to do so would have been considered as challenging the rest of the community.

On one side is an open fireplace, with a chimney running through the wall and terminating on the roof often in an old water jar whose bottom has been knocked out, and so becomes a sort of smokestack. Many houses have no chimney at all; small holes through the wall, or the windows, furnish the only exit for the smoke, which on winter days fairly fills the house.

The furniture is very simple and, as a rule, consists of a crudely decorated bridal chest in which the mother of the family has brought her trousseau; a straw mat or heavy woven woolen rug which covers part of the floor, and mattresses, with thick quilts and hard pillows, which at night are spread on the floor.

The cooking utensils are few in number— one clay cooking pot, a couple of large wooden bowls in which to knead the dough, and a couple of smaller ones used to eat from. Wheat is ground in a hand-mill of black basalt, the lower stone being imbedded in a sort of sun-dried clay trough shaped to receive the flour as it is ground. These, with a sieve or two, a large wooden cooking spoon, a small brass coffee-pot, a few tiny coffee-cups, and perhaps a clay

ROOFING A VILLAGE HOME

"The outside of the roof is covered with a coating of mortar made of clay, which, on being pressed with a small stone roller or pounded with a board, becomes hard and compact enough to shed the rain" (see page 2).

dish in which to roast and grind the coffee beans, comprise the entire outfit.

Having inspected the dwelling portion, which at once is kitchen, store-room, bedroom, and living-room, let us descend the steps into what the natives call the stable.

Below the *mastaby*, or raised platform, just described, among arches so low that a man can scarcely walk erect, are the winter quarters of the goats and sheep. To shut the flocks in, these arched entrances are obstructed with bundles of brush used as firewood for the winter. The rest of the floor space, which is open to the ceiling, is devoted to the few work cattle and perhaps a donkey or camel. Around the walls are primitive mangers for the cattle, built of rough slabs of stone placed on edge and plastered up with mortar.

Often the owner makes a small raised place on which he sleeps at night to enable him to keep better watch over the newly born lambs, lest in the crowded quarters some get crushed or trodden down by the older ones. Here he often sleeps by preference on a cold night, for he says the breath of the animals keeps him warm.

THE LAND, NOT THE PEOPLE, CONSERVES THE OLD CUSTOMS

One cannot become even tolerably acquainted with Palestine without perceiving that it is the *land* that has preserved the ancient customs. Its present-day inhabitants, who have nothing in common with the modern Jews who crowd Jerusalem, are still perpetuating the life of Abraham and the customs and ways of the people who lived here at the time of Christ.

To know the heart of the land, to have learned the hospitality of its people, which is always offered, no matter how primitive or simple, makes it easy to picture Mary and Joseph returning from the inn, already filled with guests, and turning aside into a home such as we have described, the regular dwelling portion of which may have been none too large for the family which occupied it. It may have been crowded with other guests, but they find a welcome and a resting place for the babe in a manger.

Such a use of the *rowyeh*, or stable portion of the house, by human beings is not the exception, but an every-day occurrence. You can occasionally find men working their primitive looms there or the mother preparing the food or doing her little sewing near the door, where there is more light on a dark winter's day.

We have all perhaps noticed that in the two Gospel narratives where the birth of Jesus is dwelt upon[1] neither of them mentions a stable, barn, or anything equivalent, while Matthew, speaking of the wise men, says: "And when they were come into the *house*, they saw the young child with Mary his mother."

Many of these dwellings, placed as they are on ancient sites, are built over old caves or caverns which are incorporated into the lower or stable portion. Today, in Bethlehem's church, such a cave is shown as the actual birthplace of Jesus. Its walls are covered with costly tapestries and paintings, and from its ceiling hang lamps of gold and silver (see page 52).

THE GUEST-CHAMBER OF THE VILLAGE

Each village has an upper room or guest-chamber. During the summer the shade of some large tree is often substituted for this room. However, in either case this guest-chamber

1. Matt. 2:1-12; Luke 2:1-20.

or tree is the social center for all the village men, where many spend the evening or the entire day when they have nothing with which to occupy themselves. Sociability is one of their characteristics; they love to gossip and chat about the local news. Of course, not a single newspaper is to be had; so all their information is derived from those who have been last to town.

A servant is hired to attend to this guest-chamber, and every day, by turn, one of the villagers furnishes the coffee beans and sugar for the coffee to be served to the men thus congregated; he, too, supplies the food and bedding if some ordinary guests come along.

They are, of course, great respecters of persons; so that if a common man happens in, a couple of fried eggs with bread and olives will do for him. If a more important personage arrives, a pair of roast chickens is provided for his supper; but if a still more honored one, a sheik of a village, or a large company of men appear, a lamb or kid is killed, and in all cases horses are furnished with nose-bags full of barley. The supplying of these more expensive meals is apportioned among the various men by turn, while they furnish barley according to the amount of land possessed.

In the possession of the man attending the guest-chamber are three small wooden bows, on the cord of which are strung slips of paper, each bearing the name of one of the men of the village. The slip first in order indicates the name of the person whose turn next comes to serve, and in this simple way the proper accounts are kept, since one of the bows represents chickens, the next lambs and kids, while the third is for the barley. As each one fulfills his obligation the paper representing it is torn off, and

when all are gone, a new set is written and the turns begin again.

Let us now watch a company of distinguished visitors arrive at the village guest-chamber.

The young men run to help the guests dismount, and, leading the animals away, tie them in the courtyard or in the stable, which is below the "upper room." Others hasten to spread rugs and mats on the floor and mattresses around the wall, furnished with cushions, for on them the guests sit cross-legged or recline. Many of the men of the village now join the guests, and for a while there are long exchanges of salutations, while tiny cups of coffee are sipped, and the more they enjoy it, the louder they smack their lips.

Bitter coffee is generally offered and is served with only a sip at the bottom of a very small cup, while when sweet coffee is made, the cups are filled to overflowing. This, as will be readily seen, has a symbolical meaning—"May bitterness be little and sweetness abundant."

AN INGENIOUS INSULT

Traveling with a friend some years ago, we were thus entertained. Entering the guest-chamber, we noticed that the occupants were unusually quiet and that one man had no turban on. It was whispered to us that this man, who was a stranger, had been robbed the night before by one of the men of the village who had a notoriously bad reputation, even among his own people. The victim had appealed to the elders of the town. Without a word, coffee was prepared.

As we were foreigners, they made sweet coffee for us, thinking we would not like the bitter, and filled our cups full, while the bitter kind was passed to all the rest in little doles; but to

THERE ARE NO SUFFRAGETTES HERE

The proper etiquette of the Holy Land bids the wife follow meekly on foot while her husband rides majesti-
cally in front. In the good old days the gentle sex never was seen riding, but the modern spirit is creeping in,
and "today it is a common sight to find a woman astride of a donkey" (see text, page 10).

6

the man suspected of robbery a full cup was served. This was such an insult that he flew out of the room; a fight ensued, his house was searched and the goods recovered, and the stranger again donned his headgear, which was among the things that had been stolen.

As they thus sit chatting and drinking coffee they also smoke. Each man carries a leathern pouch of tobacco from which he rolls his own cigarettes or fills a long-tubed water-pipe or nargheli.

Little preparation is made for the mid-day meal. Some hot bread, a plate of fried eggs, another of curdled milk, or a dish of fresh butter with a pile of fine sugar on top, suffices. This meal is for the guests alone.

A FEAST FOR THE STRANGER

The person whose turn it is to give the supper does not start preparations till the flocks come home in the evening, when a fatling is slain, cut into pieces, and boiled as a stew in a great kettle. Another large pot of rice is cooked.

All the men of the village now slowly congregate at the guest-chamber, each throwing down on the coat, spread for this purpose, a couple of thin loaves of bread that he has brought with him.

When all are assembled, the pile of bread is torn up into small pieces and placed in large wooden bowls. Over this, in each bowl, a large pile of rice is put and the meat on top, while a liberal supply of the gravy is added.

Sitting on the floor, first the guests, with the older and more important men, fall into circles around the bowls, and before partaking each one says *Bismallah* (in the name of Allah), to drive away the genii. With the aid of the thumb and first two fingers, great balls of rice

and soaked bread are made, which are dexterously popped into the mouth.

The food is eaten very hot, and it is surprising how much one man can consume when at such a feast and how little it takes to sustain him ordinarily.

As each set finishes eating they wash their hands, water being poured on them by a servant, as we read of in Old Testament times.[2] Then they drink coffee and smoke until time to retire, when beds are spread on the floor for the guests, some of the villagers remaining with them, sleeping in their coats. The party usually leaves the village early the next morning.

The guest-chambers are not for women; so, if a man is traveling with his family, he does not go to this regular reception place, but waits about the village until some one passing invites him into his house. This happens today just as in the case of the Levite of old who was traveling with his concubine and servant from Bethlehem-judah, and was entertained at Gibeah by the old man from Mount Ephraim who found them waiting in the street of the city.[3]

CONCERNING FAMILY LIFE

Children in the peasant family are always welcome, girl babies sometimes excepted. The father prides himself on his boys, and even the mother prefers them, and, when questioned as to the number of her offspring, she will invariably say that she has five *children* and two girls, or as many as the case may be.

Not to have a boy is a great hardship to the family and is especially felt by the mother, for

2. 2 Kings 3:11.
3. Judges 19:15-21.

WOMEN OF SAMARIA

The Samaritan woman wears the bloomers of the North under the loose long robe, or *tobe*, of the South, her costume emphasizing her geographical position. The graceful carriage of the Syrian woman is due to her custom of bearing heavy loads upon her head.

failure to have a son may become the cause of her divorce or her husband's excuse for marrying again. This feeling is hard to understand, since they look upon a girl as a profitable possession, for a would-be husband must pay a comparatively handsome price for her. The boy, on the other hand, is a greater expense, and his wife and wedding are costly affairs. The only explanation is that their great aim in life is to perpetuate the name of the father.

To be polite the *fellah*, in speaking of a pig, dog, donkey, or anything out of good taste, invariably says, *b'eed 'annak*, meaning, "Be it far from you!" So, also, when a girl or woman is spoken of, they often say, "Be it far from you!"

Although women are thus looked upon as something inferior, still when they have become well advanced in years and are perhaps the grandmothers of large families, or have signalized themselves by some special attainment, they are frequently the object of the respect and reverence of the younger women and of the men as well (see page 13).

The woman may never call her husband by his first name, but "O father of Ahmed," or

AN UNUSUAL SIGHT

From time immemorial the task of furnishing the village with water has fallen to the lot of the women, who can be seen morning and evening returning from the stream or well with their water-pots on their heads. in exceptional instances the men bring the water on the backs of donkeys and camels, as shown in the picture.

whatever the eldest son's name may be, which indeed is the name by which he is generally known.

In naming the first son it is customary to give him the name of his grandfather on the father's side; therefore, even before a youth is married he will often be addressed as the father of Ali, or Mohammed, or Suleiman, as the case may be. The first daughter is usually named for the grandmother, again on the father's side.

The wife likewise takes the name of her first-born son. The husband, speaking of her, especially to men, will never say "my wife" or mention her first name, but will say either "the mother of Ahmed," or "my family," "the relative in my house," "the forbidden," or "the daughter of my uncle."

The reason for this is that a man marries his first cousin in preference to any one else, and in fact she cannot marry another if he wants her. Gauged by our conception of the subject, the women are rigorously ruled by the men; still the men feel that in these days the women are becoming too independent, as what follows will illustrate.

ESSA'S LAMENTATION

Only yesterday Essa, who tends the vineyard of a friend near the village of Sharafat, lying between Jerusalem and Bethlehem, was heard thus complaining to another:

"Oh! my master, when I was young I used to rule 'my family' with a hard heart, for her ways did not please my mother, and I used to beat her much. My father, may God have mercy upon him,[4] often said to me: 'My son, these are the days of women, and if you so treat your wife you will not be able to live with any woman. Their ways are perverse, but you cannot change them. The days of men are passed.'

"In former days, my master, a woman would not dare to go to her father's house or that of a neighbor for a visit without first getting her husband's consent, and much less would she think of addressing her husband before people. If he happened to be in the village guest-chamber with the men and she desired to call him, she would say to some man sitting by, 'Tell *him* to come,' and sometimes, to amuse ourselves, the man would inquire, 'Who?'; to which she would repeatedly answer only, 'he,' for modesty would prevent her mentioning his name or saying 'my husband'; but now my woman calls me 'Essa' in the midst of the village and I hold my peace.

"Women formerly, when passing men on the road, would cover their faces with their hands and keep their eyes on the ground; but now when we meet them they are not shy, so we men keep our eyes on the ground until they have passed.

"A common saying among the women used to be, 'O Preserver, protect me from my husband's displeasure!' Now it is reversed and we men say, 'O Preserver, protect me from my

wife's displeasure!' Women never in former times were seen riding, but today it is a common sight to find a woman astride of a donkey, and the other day I met one so mounted, and she was even singing aloud *until she caught sight of me.*"

THE BIRTH OF THE BABY

When the *fellah* or peasant child is born, its tender skin, without being washed, is rubbed with olive oil and salt. For seven consecutive days it is re-oiled, and when a week old gets its first bath and is again oiled, and each week until it is forty days old the bath is repeated. In some localities they consider it unsafe to bathe it before it is forty days old.

Into the little eyes they put drops of liquid tar, and when two days old begin the periodical application of *kohl*. This is a dye used to blacken the eyelids of not only babies, but of women and sometimes also men, and is considered both beautifying and beneficial to the eyesight. They believe the tar to be a preventive of weak eyes, and that a child who has not been salted will develop into a weakling.

How old a custom this salting is can be seen from Ezekiel's reproachful words to Jerusalem: "And as for thy nativity, in the day thou wast born . . . thou wast not salted at all, nor swaddled at all."[5]

Swaddling clothes like those of Bible times[6] are still in use. A small shirt is the only real garment put on, around which may be wrapped some old rags, care being taken to keep the arms tightly pressed against the sides.

---

4. This expression is always used when speaking of a deceased relative or friend, while when mentioning an enemy or evil person they say, "May God not have mercy upon him!"

5. Ezekiel 16:4.
6. Luke 2:7.

THE VILLAGE MOTHER: PALESTINE

"A cap, perhaps decorated with a blue bead or some charm to keep off spirits and the evil eye, completes its apparel." The child shown here has outgrown the swaddling clothes.

A cap, perhaps decorated with a blue bead or some charm to keep off spirits and the evil eye, completes the apparel (see page 11).

When one looks at a child, before admiring it or speaking of it, in order to avert a calamity, one must say *Bismallah* (in the name of Allah), or "May Allah encircle you!" or "May the evil eye be frustrated!"

Mortality among the babies is great and is not to be wondered at, for in view of the rough treatment they receive, it becomes a question of the survival of the fittest.

HOW THE BABY IS CARRIED

In the Judean mountain districts a cradle is often kept for the baby while at home, and a sort of small hammock is used to carry the child around in when out-of-doors. The mother when going to work in the fields will be found with this hammock, called *hiddil* in Arabic, on her back suspended by a rope which passes across her forehead, often with nothing indicating that life is in it except an occasional squeal from one end.

It is a common sight when passing through the bazars to find a baby in this sling hung on a small nail or on the lock or bolt of a turned-back chop door, while the mother sits in the street behind the basket of produce she is selling, seemingly unmindful of her child's hazardous position.

When in the fields she erects a tripod of sticks, from which she suspends the hammock, and she protects it from the rays of the sun by covering it with one of her garments.

In the Samaria district and along the plain of Sharon a crudely decorated wooden cradle is the fashion and is carried by the mother on her head wherever she goes.

We cannot refrain from narrating a story heard from an eyewitness.

THE GENII CAPTURE A BABY. A TRUE STORY

A woman of Abou Shoushey,[7] waking up late one morning and picking up the cradle in haste, started off for the harvest fields.

She had no more than entered the narrow path between the stretches of standing grain when she felt her babe leap from the cradle on her head and heard it glide rapidly through the wheat.

Terror-stricken and trembling, she screamed for help, calling to the men to pursue the genii that had taken her babe.

After a heated chase some returned to inquire further particulars of her.

Unable to get a reply, for she still stood screaming, "The genii have taken my boy!" they lowered the cradle from her head and found the child still sound asleep.

The others soon returned to say they had overtaken the supposed enemy, only to find that it was her domestic cat, which had jumped from its hiding place near the baby.

HE HAD THREE DAUGHTERS BUT NO CHILDREN

Essa met us at the gate one evening and his face showed that something out of the ordinary had occurred. After the usual salutations he said, "I come to you for the reward of good news."

"And what is it?"

"My *family* gave birth to a baby."

7. Abou Shoushey is ancient Gezer, which was given by Pharaoh as a dowry to his daughter when she married King Solomon.

THE JERICHO MEDICINE WOMAN

Although women are looked upon as something inferior, still, when they have signalized themselves by some special attainment, they are frequently the object of respect and reverence. The Jericho women dress like the Bedouin, but live in villages.

"*Imbarak*" (May it be a blessing!); to which came his reply, "*Imbarak feek*" (A blessing by your presence!).

"What is it, Essa?" He hung his head and replied, "Be it far from you, a girl."

"How many children does this make?" he was asked. Essa looked embarrassed, and said, "I have no children; this is my third girl. When I went into the village this morning both women and men said to me, '*Imbarak*, Essa! May it be granted that she die!' but I replied, 'May Allah not listen to you!' for I have become like you foreigners and I am satisfied, although I had taken upon me certain vows in case it was a boy."

THE COSTUMES OF THE WOMEN

The costumes of the women differ sufficiently in each district to enable one to distinguish readily where the wearer comes from. From the variations of the headgear one can tell whether a woman be single or married; but, although differing from one another in the details, the costumes have much in common.

The dress, called a *tobe*, is like a long loose shirt, the sleeves narrow at the shoulders and widening out something like the Japanese pattern. The front and back are made each of one width of cloth, with a gore on each side to widen the skirt. A girdle either of white linen or bright striped silk is wound around the waist and the *tobe* is pulled up a little to produce a full bosom.

This *tobe*, when for common use, is of dark-blue cloth, the bosom is covered with cross-stitch embroidery and perhaps a little on the sleeves and skirt.

In the districts north of Jerusalem the *tobe* for the bride or for gala occasions is made of heavy white linen almost covered with embroidery, the prevailing colors being dark green and red with a little orange mixed in (see page 23). Around Samaria the *tobe* is made of white cotton cloth in which are woven bright strips of red, yellow, and green.

The shoes are crude affairs, the tops being of bright red or sometimes yellow sheepskin with soles of raw cow, camel, or buffalo hide.

WEARING HER DOWRY ON HER HEAD

The headgear is of two parts: first, what we shall for convenience sake call a cap, and over it a veil. The Bethlehem women wear a high cap, in shape something like a man's *fez*, called *shatweh*, on the front of which are sewn rows of gold and silver coins.

A woman never parts with the coins from her headgear except in dire circumstances, and for her to admit that she has lost one of these is considered a great shame, for an evil meaning is put upon it. This throws a strong light upon the parable of the woman who lost one of her ten pieces of silver.[8]

The woman in the Gospel had not lost a piece of money merely valuable as a medium of exchange, but a part of her ornament and dowry, and had thus brought a reflection upon her character. So it was vital for her to recover it.

No wonder, then, she is pictured as lighting a candle, sweeping the house, and seeking diligently until she finds it, and then calling her friends and neighbors to rejoice with her.

THE CAPACIOUS, USEFUL VEIL

The veil is a large affair, some 6 feet long and 4 feet wide, and placed over the cap it covers the entire headgear, except the coins in

8. Luke 15:8, 9.

WASH DAY: NAZARETH

"Unfortunately, in the Nazareth district European materials are fast displacing the handmade goods."

front. It is considered improper for women to have their head or hair showing in public. At home they put off the veil.

Ordinary veils are made of heavy white linen, with sometimes a little embroidery, while in the districts north of Jerusalem each girl makes one almost covered with needlework, so that it will match the white embroidered *tobe* for her wedding (see page 23).

Whenever a woman lacks a basket or bag, the veil comes into use. She places what she has to carry in one end of her veil, gathers and ties it around with one corner, and places the burden on top of her head.

The story of Ruth, when Boaz says to her, "Bring the veil that thou hast upon thee, and hold it; and when she held it, he measured six measures of barley, and laid it on her: and she went into the city,"[9] clearly shows that this use of the veil is the survival of a very ancient practice.

Those not acquainted with this land of ancient customs may find themselves unable to understand how Ruth's veil could contain so much grain, because of their having in mind a veil of gauze and of small dimensions. The *khirka*, as the veil is called, is not only large and strong enough for this work, but such usage is very common down to the present day.

Nor is it only the veil that has survived, but the entire costume. Ezekiel the Prophet gives us a matchless description of the woman's attire of his day when, speaking allegorically of Jerusalem, he says:

"I clothed thee also with broidered work, and shod thee with badgers' skin, and I girded thee about with fine linen, and I covered thee with silk. I decked thee also with ornaments, and I put bracelets upon thy hands, and a chain on thy neck. And I put a jewel on thy forehead, and earrings in thine ears, and a beautiful crown upon thine head. Thus wast thou decked with gold and silver; and thy raiment was of fine linen, and silk, and broidered work."[10]

THE JEWELS OF BIBLE TIMES AND OF TODAY

Jewelry is very much prized, although it is mainly confined to heavy silver pieces.

A heavy silver chain is attached to the cap on either side and hangs down about the neck and below the chin (see page 23). A collarette made of plaited silver wire with many chains hanging from it used to be extensively worn by Bethlehem women, but is fast disappearing.

In the Hebron district the unmarried girls wear a large silver coin on their forehead. Earrings are used and silver finger-rings, with Mecca stones or glass imitations, are much prized.

Were we living much later we would find it difficult to learn the meaning of the prophet's word, "And I put . . . a beautiful crown upon thy head." The *tasseh*, a disk of wrought silver or gold which, according to the old men, used to be so common, and was worn by the women sewed to the crowns of their caps, is today almost non-existent. They can occasionally be picked up at the silversmith's, where they have been sold for the silver that is in them, but the present writer has not seen a single one in use among the peasants.

In the Nazareth district European material is fast displacing hand-made goods. Even around Jerusalem the women are taking to

9. Ruth 3:15.

10. Ezekiel 16:10-13.

shawls of foreign manufacture in place of the handsome hand-embroidered veils whose colors harmonize, which cannot be said of these shawls, with their flaming roses and pink backgrounds.

Few of these peasant women can be said to be handsome; still, they make an interesting and picturesque sight, as they walk in companies along the roads, going to town with their baskets of produce, or returning, chattering like magpies over the day's transactions.

When the road is very stony or wet, it is a common custom for them to take off their shoes to save them, placing them on top of their loaded baskets (see page 54). It takes *metaliks* (coppers) to mend shoes, but feet mend themselves.

The Bethlehem women have the reputation of being handsome. Their faces are a full oval, their complexion fairer than the ordinary *fellaheen*, often having very red cheeks, and attractive in the setting of their striking headgear. Their Nazareth sisters have gained a little less renown. Both are Christians and supposed to have a considerable strain of Crusader blood in their veins.

THE ATTIRE OF THE MEN

The clothing worn by the men is very varied, and so we will consider only the most typical. There is a long shirt made of white cotton cloth, also called a *tobe*, and in form much like the women's. Over this is a sort of gabardine made of striped goods, the waist being girt about with a leather, wool, or silk girdle. The colors are quite bright, red and yellow or black and yellow being favorites.

The headgear costs him, like the woman's with its silver attached, more than all the rest of his outfit. A low dome-like fez, with a blue silk tassel, is wound round with a turban.

This turban indicates where he comes from or his class. In the district north of Jerusalem the turban consists of a large square of white linen, with a colored border woven in; around Hebron it is of silk, golden yellow and red.

A plain white one denotes a man of letters; a plain red, that he is a dervish or holy man, and a plain green again, that he claims to be a direct descendant of Mohammed. Inside this fez is a heavy felt cap, and often between them one or two old fezzes are found, while next to the head there is still another cap of white cotton cloth. The object of these many layers is to make the headgear heavy, which is commonly believed to prevent headache.

Similarly the women with their heavily weighted caps do not remove them night or day. Between the layers of the turban the man stows away his snuff-box, jackknife, often a large pack needle, sometimes money and valuable papers if he has any. They have a witty saying to the effect that if one lacks a place of safekeeping let him make his head his custodian.

Little boys are dressed like the men, with the exception that they have no turban until about 12 years old, and when his father gives a boy his first he feels just as proud and important as any American boy over his first long pants.

The men shave their heads clean, leaving only a central topknot of long hair, and to shave the beard, once it has been allowed to grow, is considered a great disgrace. To swear by one's own beard, or the beard of the one with whom the controversy is being waged, is the usual thing, as well as bringing in that of the Prophet to add weight.

"BAB-SITNA-MIRIAM": JERUSALEM

This gate is called by the Arabs the "Gate of Our Lady Mary," and is otherwise known as St. Stephen's Gate. The lions that appear are said to have been placed here by the masons to commemorate the meeting of the two gangs of workmen at this point on the completion of this wall.

The trick of shaving off half the beard of an opponent as a sign of contempt is practiced even today among the peasants exactly as it was in the days of King David when he sent his servants to Hanun, king of Ammon.[11]

AN OVERCOAT, CARRY-ALL, AND BED-CLOTHES COMBINED

The top garment or overcoat of the *fellah* is of coarse, woolen cloth woven in broad stripes of black and white or dark blue and white. In some districts the men do the spinning themselves in their spare time, take the yarn to the village weaver to be converted into cloth, and then the women sew them.

This coat is as simple in form as it is possible to be. It is nearly square and in length extends a little below the knees, is open down the front, and has an opening in each upper corner to pass the arms through. The best of them are made of only one piece of cloth, the width of which is the length of the coat, so that the only seams required are along the shoulders.

Such a garment undoubtedly was the "coat" over which at the crucifixion the Roman soldiers "cast lots" rather than "rend it," for it "was without seam woven from the top throughout."[12]

It serves as a kind of carry-all, the wearer carrying various things in it; on rainy days it is pulled up over the head and sheds the rain fairly well, and at night it is the covering in which he sleeps.

It is strange how fond both men and women are of keeping their heads well wrapped up in cold and wet weather, both when walking and sleeping, while the feet and legs can be quite

bare and exposed to the cold and wet with seemingly but little discomfort.

When the native men travel and night overtakes them far from a village, they lie down in an open field or by the roadside, thrust the head into one corner of the *abayeh*, and, wrapping it round the body, have little care whether the legs be bare or not. It is quite common to see men thus sleeping with a stone for a pillow, just as Jacob did of old at Bethel.[13]

In the Mosaic law we read: "If thou at all take thy neighbor's raiment to pledge, thou shalt deliver it unto him by that the sun goeth down: for that is his covering only: it is his raiment for his skin: wherein shall he sleep?"[14] Today the giving of small articles as a pledge or security is quite common; still, any one taking an *abayeh* from a poor man to deprive him of it overnight is considered as unmerciful and a kind of Shylock.

THE OLDEST EXISTING TYPE OF HEAD-DRESS

In some districts or villages the men wear the Bedouin headgear, consisting of a large square of cloth called *kaffeyeh*. It is doubled cornerwise, laid on the head, and held in place by an *'agal*, a thick double coil made of wool or goats' hair and black in color. The variations of this *'agal*, or coil, show from where the person comes (see page 20).

It is probable that this form of head-gear is the oldest of those now in use in the country. A small Canaanitish figure in pottery, dating back to about the 14th century B. C., now in the Whiting collection at Yale, although of necessity very crude, has such a band around the

11. 2 Samuel 10:4-5.
12. John 19:23-24.

13. Genesis 28:11.
14. Exodus 22:26, 27.

THE ROAD TO JERICHO

The two Bedouins in the foreground are wearing their characteristic head-dress, the white cloth and double coil of goats' hair. This is reputed to be one of the oldest known forms of headgear still in use and has been traced back to the fourteenth century before Christ (see page 19).

TREADING OUT THE GRAIN

"Threshing by the primitive methods employed is the most tiresome task of all the *fellah's* round of toil. In many places it is done entirely by treading out beneath the feet of the animals, which are tied together abreast and driven round and round over the spread-out grain. The mules and horses are provided with flat sheet-iron shoes for all kinds of work, and the cattle, just as the threshing season begins, are specially shod" (see page 37).

head, and shows how very ancient is the origin of this *kaffeyeh* and *'agal*.

Among certain Bedouin at the death of a woman these *'agals* are removed from the head and placed on the corpse as it is being carried from the tent to the grave; and in the Book of Ezekiel a "tire" is twice mentioned[15] as part of a man's headgear, and he was told by God that his wife was about to be taken away with a stroke; but he was not to mourn or weep, but to "bind the tire of his head upon him." This leads us to suppose that the "tire" of that time must have been the same in principle as the present-day *'agal*.

THE MARRIAGE CUSTOMS OF THE HOLY LAND

The villagers of Palestine are mostly of the Mohammedan faith, while fewer in number are the Christians belonging to the Catholic and Greek Orthodox churches. Some villages are entirely Christian, and there are a few which have both religions represented, but in this case each class has its own quarter.

We are, throughout these descriptions of the life of the present inhabitants of the Holy Land, devoting our observations to the Mohammedans, who are not only by far the most numerous, but also, from our standpoint, the more interesting, as they follow the ancient customs more closely than the Christians.

Marriage takes place at an early age, the young men at about 20 and the girls between 12 and 16. So long as the father is living, the burden and expenses of marrying his sons fall on his shoulders.

When a youth has reached a marriageable age and the expenses that a wedding involves

can be defrayed, he begins in a business-like manner to look for a bride. When his choice seems to rest upon a certain girl from simply seeing her in the village, for no courtship is allowed, or if a girl is heard of in another hamlet that strikes his fancy, then the mother of the bridegroom, with a retinue of her daughters and women friends, goes to see the prospective bride.

If she is from another village, they may spend a couple of days "looking her over," as the expression is, learning whether she bakes well and is handy at all kinds of work, seeing if she is good looking, and, above all, that her eyes are perfect. One who, like Leah of old, is "tender-eyed,"[16] is but little sought after.

FIXING THE PRICE OF THE BRIDE

The young man, with his father, uncles, and other male relatives and friends, next makes a visit. They formally ask for the girl's hand. It would be considered impolite for the girl's father to meet the request with a refusal, for if he objects to this suitor, he will not agree to the amount to be paid for her. The groom's father then offers for the bride a sum far in excess of what he really expects to give, thereby exhibiting his generosity; but this is only byplay.

Different men present urge that for their sakes the price be lessened by a certain sum, and so on until the amount is brought down to what the bride is actually known to be worth—that is, to about the habitual price. This offer being finally accepted by the father of the girl and the details of the betrothal contract arranged, the kid or lamb which the visiting party has brought with them is killed and dressed.

15. Ezekiel 24:17, 3.

16. Genesis 29:17.

THE BRIDE, PALESTINE

She is wearing her wedding dress, the white embroidered garment known as the *tobe*, and the large white veil to match,—the embroidery being all the work of her own hands. The head-dress of coins and the neck chain,— the marks of a married woman—are formed from a part of the money which her father received for her from the bridegroom. The average price of a bride is from $20 to $40.

THE VILLAGE WEDDING

"Towards evening the young men dress the bridegroom in his best and, with the entire village, go out into some open field where they have horse-racing and shooting." Note the palanquins on the camels from which the ladies of the family watch the festivities.

As these preparations are in progress, and others drop in from the village, the bridegroom or his father will rehearse the contract with the bride's father over again, so that several witnesses may hear the terms agreed upon in case of a dispute arising later. The bride has nothing to say in the matter; she is not consulted.

WHAT A BRIDE IS WORTH

The price of a bride depends on her age, beauty, usefulness, and the family to which she belongs. The daughter of an influential sheik is greatly sought after and will bring many times the price given for even superior girls from families of less importance.

The prices range in sums which represent in American money from $100 to $400, besides which the minor expenses bring up the total considerably, often doubling it.

Among these the bridegroom, according to his ability, must give a present to the guest-chamber of the bride's village, a new dress to the bride's mother, and an *abayeh* (outer garment) to her father; and her oldest uncle on both her father's and mother's side must each receive a new garment with a gold coin in the pocket. He has also to provide two feasts, for which a man in average circumstances must furnish 15 fatlings.

Meantime the father of the bride has given her from the money paid as her price, say from $20 to $40, with part of which she gets the proper coins and with them makes her first married woman's headgear. With the rest she buys a couple of pairs of bracelets, some finger-rings, and an *iznak*, or neck chain.

The balance of the money the father keeps, just as if he had sold some cattle or produce, except that it is the custom for him to give her

an every-day *tobe*, or dress, a veil, and a mattress, pillow, and quilt.

THE BRIDE LEAVES HER NATIVE VILLAGE

From the time the trousseau is bought until the actual wedding day, a period from a week to 10 days, there will be dancing every night in the guest-chamber by the men, while the women make merry in the bridegroom's home.

When the bride belongs to another village, they go for her the day before the wedding, the company consisting of the bridegroom and his men and women relatives and a lot of his young men friends, all dressed in their best and armed with whatever weapons they may possess, and many of them mounted. They take with them several sheep or goats.

Upon reaching the village, they slaughter all the animals they have brought, and the entire village partakes of the feast. The bride is now arrayed in her new costume, puts on the married woman's cap and all her jewelry, her face is covered with a green or red gauze veil, and finally there is thrown over her entire person a man's gabardine.

She is mounted on a horse or camel, and with the firing of guns, the racing of horses, and a great send off, they leave the village, the bride's mother carrying the bridal chest along on her head, she being about the only person who goes with her, except perhaps a sister or female friend.

As the bride leaves the village she receives a gold coin of about $2 in value from the villagers, which in fact is part of the amount paid by the groom to the guest-chamber, and each of her uncles gives her a present in money. In each village through which she passes on her way she is met and a piece of money given her.

DRYING STRAW BASKETS

After the baskets have been made they are laid in the hot sun to dry. The women will then carry them long distances to market, where they sell them for an amount corresponding to five cents in American money. To the Western mind this does not seem a very great reward for labor, but they are satisfied.

WHERE THE RAVENS FED ELIJAH

In a deep ravine a few miles east of Jerusalem runs the brook Cherith, alongside of which Elijah was fed by the ravens (1 Kings 17:5). The picture shows the brook as it turns the corner under the convent of St. George.

The bridal party has now arrived at the bridegroom's village, and the bride and those with her become by invitation the guests of the first house they reach, and this opportunity of entertaining them is looked upon as a distinctive honor. The host kills a fatling and prepares a feast to which only women are admitted, and here, under the protection of her mother, the bride spends her first night in her new village.

When the bride has arrived safely, messengers are sent back to invite her father and male relatives to the ensuing ceremonies, and if the groom be prominent or wealthy he calls all his friends in the surrounding country to take part in the marriage feast.

THE WEDDING CEREMONIES

Early the next morning the wholesale slaying and cooking is begun, and a special dish is prepared for the women. During the day the religious formalities are attended to with great secrecy. The bride, in the presence of two witnesses, appoints her father or nearest male relative as her representative.

The groom and the bride's representative are now seated facing each other, and a certain exact formula is thrice repeated with much punctiliousness. The parties are prompted by the *khatib* (teacher), or the religious head of the village, who does not allow the slightest mistake to pass uncorrected. In this manner the young man accepts the bride as his wife and the representative of the girl in her stead agrees that she be his wife. At this time the marriage contract is written, which gives the names of both parties, the sum paid for the bride, with all the minor details.

The explanation of the secrecy observed while the couple is thus being married is that they believe that should an enemy be present and either spill flour on the ground or tie knots in a string a specific calamity will surely befall the newly married pair.

Toward evening the young men dress the bridegroom in his best, and with the entire village go out into some open field, where they have horse-racing and shooting (see page 24), in both of which the groom is supposed to demonstrate his skill, while the women stand by and sing.

Returning to the village, the men go to the guest-chamber and the marriage supper begins, while the women congregate at the groom's home and likewise feast. A portion is also sent to the bride and another to the family where she is a guest. The details of these customs vary, however, in each district.

When the feasting is over in the guest-chamber, each guest drops a coin as a present for the groom into a handkerchief spread out for the purpose. Amid much joyous excitement a herald announces the name of each donor and the amount given, calling upon Allah to recompense him.

Meanwhile the women have taken the bride, with much rejoicing and merriment, from the house where she has been visiting to her new home, going either mounted as she came from her village or on the shoulders of two women, while in some localities she walks.

They dress her in her bridal attire, her arms and legs having been previously dyed with henna, the face is decorated with gold leaf, and the eyelashes and eyebrows blackened with *kohl*, which to the *fellah* is the acme of beauty. Her head and face are finally covered with a thin veil. The men are notified when all is ready, and with much pomp and firing of guns, they escort the

THE SHEPHERD'S SLING

"With this he becomes expert in throwing stones to a great distance and with great precision. With such a simple weapon . . . the stripling David . . . encountered Goliath and slew him" (see page 50).

THE SHEPHERD'S FLUTE

These simple pipes have been popular in the land for thousands of years and are doubtless similar to those used when Solomon was anointed. "And the people piped with pipes and rejoiced with great joy, so that the earth was rent with the sound of them" (1 Kings 1:40).

groom to his house, when all retire and he alone enters.

Removing the bride's veil and wiping off the gold leaf, they stand together, while presents of money are given to the bride by her male relatives and the women, as the groom had received his previously. The husband begins by giving his first. No men are admitted except the male relatives of the bride, and they only long enough to present the bride with their gifts.

For the first few days the bride keeps on her finery and does no work; but this luxury and immunity she does not long enjoy, for we soon find her at the regular hard work which falls to the woman's lot.

AGRICULTURE IN THE HOLY LAND

In the mountain districts the farm land is usually owned by peasant proprietors, each man's property being composed of various small pieces scattered about near the village in which

SUNRISE ON THE FLOCK

"Those unacquainted with the pastoral life of this land, who do not know the almost human relationship between the flocks and their keepers, may wonder how the sheep are separated by their different owners when morning comes. The sheep respond to the voice of their own shepherd, but, so well do they know the individual members of the flock of which they are part, that when the morning breaks each flock gathers itself together as a matter of habit" (see page 55).

he lives. The raising of olives, grapes, and many other fruits is the leading occupation, but almost every farmer grows some grain.

Down on the plains larger fields exist and cereals are largely planted. The land of a given village is frequently owned in common by the villagers, and a division of it takes place every year or every alternate year, and is so arranged that each man gets portions of the good as well as of the less desirable land.

Fences, in the western sense of the word, are unknown. In the mountainous country lands are inclosed by loose stone walls, still called by the ancient Hebrew name *jedar*, and on the plains by thorn hedges. When the open fields are owned individually, the boundary lines are indicated by deep furrows, in which at intervals stones are laid as "landmarks." It is therefore readily seen how easily these boundaries could be changed by an avaricious neighbor, undeterred by the Mosaic warning, "Cursed be he that removeth his neighbor's landmark."[17]

17. Deut. 27:17.

SISTERS

"But in the Samaria district they braid their hair in two plaits, on the ends of which hang silver tubes with small coins or ornaments attached."

IN THE CHRISTIAN QUARTER: JERUSALEM

This street is peculiar in respect to the number of projecting windows.

AN ARABIAN JEW

These Jews, claiming to be of the tribe of Gad, have lived for centuries in Yemen in Southern Arabia. They are more like the present-day inhabitants of the land than any other Jews.

LAND STILL SOLD
BY THE "YOKE" AND "REED"

Until a comparatively short time ago real estate was bought and sold by the use of a contract, which the chief men of the place witnessed and sealed; nor has this custom become entirely obsolete. Farming land is estimated by the *faddan*, which, being literally translated, is "yoke," but implies a piece of land "that a yoke of oxen might plow" in a day. (Compare 1 Samuel 14:14.) City property, on the other hand, is measured by a standard known as a "reed." We can trace its use far back into ancient times in the writings of Ezekiel and St. John.[18]

PLOWING AND PLANTING

Rain[19] begins to fall about November, after a rainless summer, and as soon as the ground is well moistened the *fellah* starts planting the winter cereals—wheat, barley, lentils, beans, etc. The plow is a crude affair, made of oak, the bent parts being natural curves held together with iron bands; these bands and a small plowshare, which only scratches the ground a few inches deep, are the only metal parts.

Oxen are the favorite animals for yoking to a plow. Cows and donkeys are employed by the poorer people. Horses, mules, and camels (the latter only along the Mediterranean coast) are harnessed singly to plows, while sometimes one sees an ox and camel yoked together. In the Bible the command was "Thou shalt not plow with an ox and ass together."[20]

The *fellah* sows the grain on the bare ground and then plows it in. In rocky ground a

man or woman follows with a pick to loosen the earth in the spots that may have been skipped by the plow. The soil is not fertilized. The disintegration of the underlying limestone feeds the soil, so that for thousands of years it has continued yielding crops.

The manure and rubbish, instead of being utilized, are allowed to accumulate in heaps outside the villages until they surround it like small mountains. Immediately a house is deserted and the roof falls in the women find it more convenient to dump their rubbish there than to go farther, and in a short time the ruined house becomes a dunghill.[21]

After the winter crops have all been planted the vineyards and olive groves are plowed a couple of times and also the fields reserved for the summer planting. These latter crops are not put into the ground until the rains have entirely ceased.

Watermelons and muskmelons, tomatoes, a species of cucumber, vegetable marrow, are all raised without a drop of rain or of water by irrigation, but are sustained by the moisture stored in the ground from the winter rains, aided by the copious summer dews. The natives consider that rain falling after the summer crops have been planted is extremely detrimental to them.

During harvest time the fields are lively and picturesque; the entire family has a part in the work, the small children playing about among the sheaves, and even the babies are brought to the fields.

A large toothed sickle is employed by the reapers when the grain is long, but if short a smaller one is used, the edge being quite dull; so that it does not cut, but simply uproots the

18. Ezekiel, 40th to 42d chaps.; Rev. 21:15, 16.
19. The annual average rainfall for the past 50 years has been 26 inches.
20. Deut. 22:10.

21. Ezra 6:11; Daniel 3:29.

THE SMILING BUTCHER

The dweller in Jerusalem has no scientific prejudices. As long as he gets his meat, it does not worry him if the delivery is effected under conditions that would horrify an American inspector of public health.

grain. Sheepskin aprons and a large glove are often worn by the men harvesters: but the women, who are doing the very same work as the men, are provided with neither.

Destitute women and girls are allowed to follow the reapers and glean the fallen ears, which they tie into neat little bundles, dropping them on the ground as they go along, and these they gather up every evening and beat out the grain with a stick, just as Ruth did of old in the fields of Bethlehem.[22]

During the reaping period what the Bible calls "parched corn" is made in almost every field. Some wheat not fully ripe is cut down and set on fire, the straw only being consumed. The roasted heads are rubbed between the hands and the chaff winnowed out in the wind. Without further preparation, this roasted wheat forms one of the common articles of diet of the reapers. Undoubtedly such was the "parched corn" which Boaz reached to Ruth.[23]

THE THRESHING-FLOOR

A large flat rock in the mountainous country or a hard piece of ground on the plains is selected for the threshing-floor, and this, up to the present time, bears the Biblical name *joren*. Here all the grain is gathered.

We read that Jacob, after his dream at Bethel, promised to God one-tenth of all he should receive.[24] Later, when this land was possessed by the Israelites, they were enjoined to give a tenth of their produce to the Levites.[25] We also find Samuel telling Israel what they could expect if they were determined to have a king to reign over them, saying: "He [the king] will take

22. Ruth 2:17.
23. Ruth 2:14; 1 Sam. 17:17 and 25:18.
24. Gen. 28:22.
25. Lev. 27:30.

the tenth of your seed, and of your vineyards, . . . and he will take the tenth of your sheep."[26]

Nor does this custom ever seem to have ceased, for the tithe is still collected. There are numerous mosques, schools, and other religious institutions which receive it from specified properties on which it is charged, and from all other tillable land it is collected by the government, the right of exacting these taxes from each village being farmed out to the highest bidder.

The sheaves are brought to the threshing floor on the backs of camels, mules, and donkeys, and in big bundles on the heads of the women, and are stacked up in the requisite number of piles. One of these is first chosen by the tax collector and has to be separately trodden out and the grain delivered to him before the rest of the work begins.

Threshing by the primitive methods employed is the most tiresome task of all the *fellah*'s round of toil. In many places it is done entirely by treading out beneath the feet of the animals, which are tied together abreast and driven round and round over the spread-out grain (see page 21).

The mules and horses are provided with flat sheet-iron shoes for all kinds of work, and the cattle, just as the threshing season begins, are specially shod. On each half of the cloven hoof a small iron shoe is nailed, and this not only facilitates the work of separating the grain, but prevents the animal from becoming lame.

HOW THE GRAIN IS WINNOWED

In the simple treading-out process the animals are driven around slowly over the grain, while the men, with wooden forks, keep stir-

26. 1 Sam. 8:15, 17.

MEASURING THE GRAIN

This is one of the scenes of the threshing floor, as primitive to-day as it was in the Biblical period 2000 years ago. It helps us to understand the phrase, "good measure, pressed down and shaken together and running over." Luke 6:38.

ring it up. When thoroughly threshed, the straw has been chopped up into short bruised bits and all is then heaped up.

To separate the grain, "the fan," which is a wooden fork, is used, the farmer waiting until the wind is blowing hard enough without being violent. Such conditions are best found in the evenings or during moonlight nights. The winnower tosses up the trampled grain into the air, and, being heavier than the straw, it falls into a heap by itself, while the fine straw separates into a neat pile a little distance away. The dust and very fine particles are completely blown away. This refuse is called *ur* by the Arabs, the original Hebrew name.

A sieve is now employed, and through this the grain is passed to take out the coarse stubble that is too heavy to be blown away. Sometimes a wooden shovel is used to give the grain a final winnowing. The presence of the stubble is accounted for by the fact that during harvest the grain is largely pulled up by the roots.

This fine straw is kept as fodder for the animals, for hay is unknown. The Arabic name for this is *tiben*, being identical with the Hebrew word which has been translated "straw," and in Bible times as now was fed to the animals or mixed into the clay when making bricks. We read in Exodus that when Pharaoh refused to give the Hebrews straw (*tiben*) to make bricks they were scattered throughout all the land to gather stubble instead.[27]

It might be interesting to note in passing that when the mounds covering the ruins of the Jericho of Joshua's time were unearthed by German explorers a few years ago the ancient bricks were found to be identical in size and texture with those made now by the inhabitants of mod-

ern Jericho, having *tiben* mixed in just in the same way.

THE THRESHING-FLOUR MOSQUE

In the southeast corner of Jerusalem, close by the city walls, is an inclosure some 30 acres in extent, in which stands the far-famed Mosque of Omar. Its graceful dome, tiled exterior, and richly decorated interior, with superb mosaics and stained-glass windows of arabesque designs, make it one of the chief attractions of Jerusalem to the tourist (see pages 42 and 44).

Besides its beauty and grandeur, the past history of the site demands attention. Thither Abraham came to sacrifice on the summit of Mount Moriah his only son, Isaac.[28] Later King David bought the threshing-floor located on this site from Ornan, the Jebtisite, and built an altar to offer sacrifice in order that the plague then raging in Israel might be stayed. "Then David said, This is the house of the Lord God, and this is the altar of the burnt offering for Israel."[29] Although David made great preparations, the actual building of the temple on this spot was left to his son Solomon.

A second temple, far less grand, was erected there by the Jews after the return from captivity in Babylon, and the third and magnificent one was reconstructed and enlarged by Herod.

After the complete destruction of Jerusalem in A. D. 70, Hadrian erected here a temple to Jupiter. Between this and the time that the present mosque was built by Abd el Melik, little is known of the history of the site.

To the Moslems this mosque, erroneously attributed to the Caliph Omar, is the most sacred shrine after the Kaaba at Mecca. Under the

---

27. Exodus 5:12.

28. Gen., ch. 22.
29. 1 Chron., chs. 21 and 22.

PICKING JAFFA ORANGES

Around the coast town of Jaffa are large orange groves, irrigated by water from numerous wells. Here are grown the Jaffa oranges which are world-famed for their size and flavor. Most of these oranges are shipped to England, where they are highly esteemed and bring good prices in the markets.

THE WALLS OF JERUSALEM

This is the northeast corner of the old city wall. Jerusalem was fortified by the Crusaders and later by Saladin in 1192. The fortifications were dismantled in 1219 and restored ten years later, only to be destroyed again in 1239. The present walls were built in 1542 by Suleiman the Magnificent.

gorgeous dome, seen only in the subdued light which filters in through matchless stained glass, is the flat rock supposed to be part of the original threshing-floor (see page 42).

THE LEGEND OF THE MOSQUE OF OMAR

The legend runs thus: Two brothers were threshing out their grain upon this floor. The older one wakes one night and sees all about him his large family of children, while his brother lies on his grain piles alone. Thus contemplating his many blessings, the abundance of the crop, his large pile of grain catches his eye, and again thinking of his bachelor brother, and wishing to add some happiness to the life of one who has no family to love and be loved by, rises and from his own pile adds a quantity to that of his brother.

After the elder brother has again fallen asleep, the younger awakes, meditates on the many bounties he should be grateful for—a full crop and health and strength—his brother and his large family attract his thoughts. He reasons that he who has no one dependent upon him could well spare some of his crop and thereby perhaps add joy to his brother's life.

BENEATH THE DOME OF THE MOSQUE OF OMAR

Under this gorgeous dome, with its superb mosaics of Arabesque design, seen only in the subdued light which filters in through the ancient stained glass windows, is a great flat rock, the summit of Mount Moriah, part of the threshing floor of Ornan, the Jebusite. 1 Chron. 21 and 22 (see also page 44).

Unwittingly he returns to his brother's pile exactly the amount that had shortly before been taken from it, and in the morning, neither knowing what the other had done, both were surprised to find their grain undiminished.

As soon as the grapes, figs, and other fruits begin ripening, the *fellah*, with his entire family, moves out of the village into the vineyard.

The grape season is looked forward to as the best part of the year, and at this time the natives live for the most part on fruits and bread. Jokingly, the *fellaheen* say that they get so fat from eating grapes that their fezzes burst.

BEATING THE OLIVE TREES

A saying among the peasants likens the vine to a city woman, for it cannot stand being neglected for a single year; the fig tree to a Bedouin woman, for it can withstand about five years of neglect, and the olive tree to a *fellaha* woman, for it is still found alive after 60 years of neglect.

This simile is given to illustrate how hardy the olive tree is as compared with the fig and the vine. To an Occidental, familiar with the almost indestructible qualities of the olive, it also serves as an example of the hardiness of the women of this sturdy mountain race.

The olives are harvested in the fall, but by a method so injurious to the trees that they yield a full crop but once in two years. Instead of picking them by hand, for time is not money with these easy-going people, they beat the trees with sticks to knock off the fruit, which at the same time results in destroying the tender shoots which should bear the next year's fruit.

When questioned, they admit the folly of this beating, but add that their fathers did so and why should they change. Evidently they are copying not only their fathers, but the Israelites before them, for we read in the Mosaic writings, "When thou *beatest* thine olive tree, thou shalt not go over the boughs again: it shall be for the stranger, for the fatherless, and for the widow."[30]

The olives when salted or pickled in brine are valued food, for a peasant can make a meal of only bread and olives, with perhaps the addition of a raw onion. The oil is a food staple, taking the place of meat. It is also, to a limited extent, burned in small clay lamps, identical in shape with those found in Canaanitish tombs, many of which were buried here before the Israelites possessed this land.

CARE OF THE POOR

A characteristic of these poor peasants is their hospitality and their kindness to the destitute.

One can any day see a party of women coming to town with their baskets for the market, and as they pass the beggars sitting by the roadside, they drop them a bit of bread or a little of the produce brought in for sale, and frequently the donor will be seemingly as poor as the receiver.

One of the prettiest, perhaps, of all Arabic words is the one for bread, namely, *aish*, meaning life, for with them it is veritably the "staff of life." Bread is looked upon as almost sacred, and they will never allow a crumb to fall where it will be trodden upon, and if a fragment is found dropped, perhaps by some child, on the ground it is lifted and kissed and laid up on a wall or put into a crack where some animal or fowl may find it.

The village home has near it a small hut containing the oven, called the *taboon*. It is a dome some 3 to 4 feet in diameter, made by the

30. Deut. 24:20.

JERUSALEM IN A WINTER STORM

The great dome, which stands out so prominently, is that of the Mosque of Omar, which covers the site of the threshing floor of Oman, the Jebusite. (See also page 42.) This is one of the most sacred spots in the world, the place where Abraham was ready to offer up Isaac; where David sacrificed to stay the plague and where Solomon built his great temple. The Mosque of Omar ranks among the Moslems as second only in sanctity to the Kaaba at Mecca.

women, of clay, with an opening in the top and is provided with a cover of the same material. It stands on the ground, slightly raised by stones beneath its rim. In the bottom is a thick layer of loose pebbles. It is heated by banking up around the outside a quantity of hot ashes.

After the day's baking the woman adds as fuel some dried manure or stubble, which ignites from the hot ashes and keeps smouldering, and so heats the oven for the next day's

baking. Bread is made from soft and elastic dough. The woman brings a bowl of it to the *taboon*, makes a rather thin loaf by throwing a piece of the dough from hand to hand, and then flops it on to the pebbles at the bottom of the oven.

About six of these loaves fill the oven, and when baked they are full of the indentations made by the small stones. When well made and eaten warm, this bread is very good.

THE SPINNING WOMAN

This woman belongs to a class like that of the people of Jericho, neither Bedouin nor peasant, but a compound of both. Her costume, like her blood, is a mixture, her dress is Bedouin in character but her head-dress is similar to that worn by the peasant women.

ON THE WAY TO THE WELL

"Women formerly, when passing men on the roads, would cover their faces with their hands and keep their eyes on the ground but now when you meet them they are not shy." It will be noted that the woman on the extreme left observes the more modest custom.

MAKING OLIVE OIL

"A piece of an ancient column serves as a roller, the olives being placed on a rock and crushed by passing this stone back and forth over them." Note the rich blue black color of the ripe olive.

THE GARDEN OF GETHSEMANE

The garden of Gethsemane is now in charge of the Capuchins, an order of Franciscan friars belonging to the Roman Catholic Church. They tend it with the greatest care and it is one of the beauty spots of the Holy Land. It contains a few olive trees of great age, some of which are believed to have been in existence at the time of Christ.

"THE MOTHER OF ALL TURTLES"

A story is told of a woman who refused to allow her neighbor to bake some dough in her *taboon*. The neighbor then begged the loan of a loaf of bread, to be returned as soon as she baked, for her oven was still too cool and her boy crying from hunger.

This was also refused, which so called down the wrath of the Almighty that an angel was sent, who, lifting up the hot *taboon*, or oven, placed it on the back of the merciless woman, leaving only the limbs and the head protruding.

So she who thus refused bread became the mother of all turtles, and if you seem to doubt it, the *fellah* will prove it to you by calling your attention not only to the fact that the turtle's shell resembles the *taboon* in shape, but also to the markings on the top of the shell like the pebbles used in the oven.

THE UPPER ROOM

"To make use of the *rowyeh*, or stable portion of the house, by human beings is not the exception but an everyday occurrence. . . . Many of these dwellings, placed as they are on ancient sites, are built over old caves or caverns which are incorporated with the lower or stable portion." (See text.)

The shells of small turtles are much in vogue as charms, by peasants and city people alike, and are often to be seen strung on a cord along with blue beads, a bit of alum, etc., and worn by the children.

A story told by a peasant living at Artas, where King Solomon had his gardens,[31] runs thus: A certain *fellah* living by the seaside was in the habit of feeding every day a loaf of bread to a whale. The chief of the genii noticed it and, addressing him, said: "For your kindheartedness you shall be rewarded. Gold and riches you can obtain by working for them, but I will give you something you cannot otherwise get. You shall have the gift of understanding the animals, but mind you do not tell any one about it."

When he returned home with his tired oxen from the day's plowing he heard the donkey say to one of the oxen, "If only you would not eat your food the master would think you were sick and would not take you out to plow."

Hearing this the man began laughing, and his wife asked the reason, but he did not tell her. The next morning, to repay the donkey for his intriguing, he hitched him to the plow instead of the ox. When he was brought back in the evening the ox asked him how he liked plowing. He pretended not to be tired, but advised the ox that if he continued not eating, the master would slaughter him.

The farmer, hearing this, laughed heartily, but would not reply to his wife's queries as to the reason of seemingly laughing at nothing. Next morning he took out the ox to plow, and the beast, fearing that the man might be leading him away to slaughter, as the donkey had said, pulled back and did not want to move. The

man, knowing the reason, again began to laugh, which so aroused his wife's curiosity that she insisted if he did not tell her the cause of his amusement it was because he did not love her.

After much importuning, he at last told her the whole story, and no sooner had he done so than he lost this peculiar gift and could no longer understand the language of the animals.

HOW DAVID SLEW GOLIATH

Some experience as a shepherd befalls almost every peasant boy whose family has flocks.

As he watches over the feeding sheep, he cuts a little wool from the back of one, spins it with the aid of only a smooth pebble, and then converts the yarn into a sling such as is always carried in the scrip.

With this he becomes expert in throwing stones to a great distance and with much precision. It not only serves as a weapon of defense, but when a sheep or goat wanders off and will not return at his call he will drop a stone near it, and this at once has the desired effect.

With such a simple weapon, and a stone taken from his shepherd's bag, which was undoubtedly similar to the one above described. it will be remembered the stripling David, while still caring for his father sheep, encountered Goliath, the Philistine giant, and slew him[32] (see page 29).

When the owner of a flock has no son to care for the sheep, he hires a shepherd, and not only feeds him, but supplies a stipulated amount of clothing and shoes. The wages paid in money amount to only a few dollars a year.

It is not uncommon for a shepherd or a plowman thus serving a master to receive, instead of wages, one of the man's daughters as a

31. Eccl. 2:5.

32. 1 Sam. 17:40, 49.

STREET SCENE IN BETHLEHEM

Bethlehem stands in the midst of a fertile district producing an abundance of wheat, barley, olives, vegetables and grapes and in consequence its market is always well supplied. Since 1834, when the entire Moslem colony was destroyed by Ibrahim Pasha after an insurrection, there have been comparatively few Moslems among its inhabitants.

THE GROTTO OF THE NATIVITY

"To-day, in Bethlehem's church, such a cave is shown as the actual birthplace of Jesus. Its walls are covered with costly tapestries and from its ceiling hang lamps of gold and silver." The church over the grotto was built by the Empress Helena, the mother of Coastantine the Great.

wife, just as Jacob contracted with Laban for his two daughters, Leah and Rachel.[33] The usual time served for a wife is from five to seven years.

PRIMITIVE METHODS OF DAIRYING

As long as the flocks are kept in the village, the sheep, as well as the goats, are milked by the women, and the milk turned into cheese and butter, to be sold in the city markets.

33. Gen. 29:15-29.

Butter is made in a goat skin like those used for carrying water. This is only half filled with the milk, which previously has been allowed to sour. The skin is blown full of air, the opening tied up, and it is hung on a tripod of sticks and shaken back and forth by one or two women until the butter is formed.

We have no record of how the ancient shepherds of this land made their butter, but could it have been by a cruder or more primitive process? This butter is quite white, and is

THE VILLAGE CARPENTER

Each village in Palestine has a carpenter who repairs the ploughs and receives in exchange from each farmer a stipulated amount of grain. Note the primitive tools and the great toe used to hold the wood.

ON THE WAY TO MARKET

Like all Orientals these peasant women carry their produce to market on their heads. It is a common custom with them to take off their shoes and place them on top of their loaded baskets. The woman on the left is practising this form of economy.

not eaten, spread on bread, as with us, but is mostly converted into a cooking requisite by boiling until all the watery parts have evaporated, when it is stored in goat skins, and keeps indefinitely.

Fresh butter is also eaten served in a bowl, with usually a quantity of sugar, honey, or molasses made of grapes added,[34] in which each dips their morsel of bread.

34. Isaiah 7:15, 22.

During the day each shepherd pastures his flock independently, but in the evening all meet at the selected rendezvous. It may be a large open field or a spot where they are protected from the wind. Here all the flocks intermix in one great company during the night.

The shepherds arrange among themselves for a watch, each set of four or five men keeping guard for an hour or two, while the rest sleep curled up in their sheepskin. Sometimes they stand like sentinels over the sheep in

IN A JERUSALEM MARKET

This market, known as the *Bab-khan-el-Zeit*, is the chief one in the old Moslem Quarter. The different faiths and races in the Holy City dwell more or less apart and each patronize separate markets.

the solitude of the still, starlit night, just like the shepherds of old on the first Christmas eve.

CALLING THE SHEEP BY NAME

Those unacquainted with the pastoral life of this land, who do not know the almost human relationship between the flocks and their keepers, may wonder how the sheep are separated by their different owners when morning comes.

The sheep respond to the voice of their own shepherd, but, so well do they know the individual members of the flock of which they are part, that when the morning breaks each flock gathers itself together as a matter of habit. Then the shepherds start off in different directions, each calling his own sheep, sometimes standing on a rock or elevated place, and the sheep prick up their ears and look around, and seeing their shepherd, follow him because they know his voice.

The shepherd, to make sure that none is left behind, causes his flock to pass under his rod between him and a rock, and as they pass he counts them.[35]

As a rule, when the shepherd calls one by its name it will answer with a bleat or come running expecting a treat, as a bit of bread from his scrip or a twig of leaves broken from a tree.

Each shepherd carries a club or crook, and uses it for defense and protection and not, as in other countries, to drive the sheep with, for here the shepherd always precedes the flock and they follow him. In case of danger, such as the intrusion of some wild animal, the sheep rush to him, and this weapon on his shoulder seems to allay their fears, reminding one of the words, "Thy rod and thy staff they comfort me."[36]

To know these shepherds is to understand how the Shepherd Psalmist and King, contemplating all the incidents and vicissitudes of his pastoral life, could compose that matchless psalm, of such solace and strength, "The Lord is my shepherd, I shall not want."[37]

35. Lev. 27:32.

36. Psalm 23:4.
37. Psalm 23:1.

IMPRESSIONS OF PALESTINE

BY JAMES BRYCE

BRITISH AMBASSADOR TO THE UNITED STATES, 1906-1913

NO COUNTRY has been so often described or so minutely described by travelers of all sorts of tastes and interests as Palestine has been; and this is natural, for none has excited so keen an interest for so long a time and in so many nations.

As we have all at some time or other read much about the country, it may well be thought that nothing now remains to be said about Palestine, except by archeologists, whose explorations of the sites of ancient cities are always bringing fresh facts to light. But if all of us have read a good deal about the Holy Land, most of us have also forgotten a good deal, and our ideas of the country—ideas colored by sentiments of reverence and romance—are often vague and not always correct.

It may therefore be worth while to set down in a plain and brief way the salient impressions which the country makes on a Western traveler who passes quickly through it. The broad impressions are the things that remain in memory when most of the details have vanished, and broad impressions are just what an elaborate description sometimes fails to convey, because they are smothered under an infinitude of details.

A SMALL COUNTRY

Palestine is a tiny little country. Though the traveler's handbooks prepare him to find it small, it surprises him by being smaller than he expected. Taking it as the region between the Mediterranean on the west and the Jordan and Dead Sea on the east, from the spurs of Lebanon and Hermon on the north to the desert at Beersheba on the south, it is only 110 miles long and from 50 to 60 broad—that is to say, it is smaller than New Jersey, whose area is 7,500 square miles.

Of this region large parts did not really belong to ancient Israel. Their hold on the southern and northern districts was but slight, while in the southwest a wide and rich plain along the Mediterranean was occupied by the warlike Philistines, who were sometimes more than a match for the Hebrew armies. Israel had, in fact, little more than the hill country, which lay between the Jordan on the east and the maritime plain on the west. King David, in the days of his power, looked down from the hill cities of Benjamin, just north of Jerusalem, upon Philistine enemies only 25 miles off, on the one side, and looked across the Jordan to Moabite enemies about as far off, on the other.

Nearly all the events in the history of Israel that are recorded in the Old Testament happened within a territory no bigger than the State of Connecticut, whose area is 4,800 square miles; and into hardly any other country has there been crowded from the days of Abraham till our own so much history—that is to say, so many events that have been recorded and deserve to be recorded in the annals of mankind. To history, however, I shall return later.

FEELING PALESTINE'S SMALLNESS

Nor is it only that Palestine is really a small country. The traveler constantly feels as he moves about that it is a small country. From the heights a few miles north of Jerusalem he sees, looking northward, a far-off summit carrying snow for eight months in the year. It is Hermon, nearly 10,000 feet high—Hermon, whose fountains feed the rivers of Damascus.

But Hermon is outside the territory of Israel altogether, standing in the land of the Syrians; so, too, it is of Lebanon. We are apt to think of that mountain mass as within the country, because it also is frequently mentioned in the Psalms and the Prophets; but the two ranges of Lebanon also rise beyond the frontiers of Israel, lying between the Syrians of Damascus and the Phoenicians of the West.

Perhaps it is because the maps from which children used to learn Bible geography were on a large scale that most of us have failed to realize how narrow were the limits within which took place all those great doings that fill the books of Samuel and Kings. Just in the same way the classical scholar who visits Greece is surprised to find that so small a territory sufficed for so many striking incidents and for the careers of so many famous men.

LITTLE NATURAL WEALTH

Palestine is a country poor in any natural resources. There are practically no minerals, no coal, no iron, no copper, no silver, though recently some oil wells have been discovered in the Jordan Valley. Neither are there any large forests, and though the land may have been better wooded in the days of Joshua than it is now, there is little reason to think that the woods were of trees sufficiently large to constitute a source of wealth. A comparatively small area is fit for tillage.

To an Arab tribe that had wandered through a barren wilderness for 40 weary years, Canaan may well have seemed a delightful possession; but many a county in Iowa, many a department in France, could raise more grain or wine than all the Holy Land.

PLAIN OF ESDRAELON

There is one stretch of fertile, level land 20 miles long and from 3 to 6 miles wide—the Plain of Esdraelon. But with this exception it is only in the bottoms and on the lower slopes of a few valleys, chiefly in the territory of Ephraim from Bethel northward and along the shores of the Bay of Acre, that one sees cornfields and olive yards and orchards. Little wine is now grown.

VILLAGERS VISITING THE TOMB OF MOSES

Although Holy Writ tells us that the Lord buried Moses "in the land of Moab, over against Beth-peor," and that "no man knoweth his sepulcher unto this day," thousands of pilgrims annually visit what they believe to be his tomb.

THE DAMASCUS GATE:
ONE OF THE PRINCIPAL ENTRANCES TO THE OLD CITY AT JERUSALEM

The view from the top of. Damascus Gate is one of the most striking in Jerusalem. From it one may see the Church of the Holy Sepulchre, Mount Zion, the Tower of David, the Mosque of Omar, the Mount of Olives, and the gilded domes of the Russian Church, which proclaim Gethsemane.

Such wealth as the country has consists in its pastures, and the expression "a land flowing with milk and honey" appropriately describes the best it has to offer, for sheep and goats can thrive on the thin herbage that covers the hills, and the numerous aromatic plants furnish plenty of excellent food for the bees; but it is nearly all thin pasture, for the land is dry and the soil mostly shallow. The sheep and goats vastly out-number the oxen. Woody Bashan, on the east side of Jordan, is still the region where one must look for the strong bulls.

SEEN THROUGH A GOLDEN HAZE

Palestine is not a beautiful country. The classical scholar finds charms everywhere in Greece, a land consecrated to him by the ge-nius of poets and philosophers, although a great part of Greece is painfully dry and bare. So, too, the traveler who brings a mind suffused by rev-

THRESHING-FLOOR SCENE IN THE FIELDS OF BOAZ, NEAR BETHLEHEM

The trampled grain is tossed into the air; the fine straw separates into a neat pile by itself, while the dust and very fine particles are completely blown away.

PALESTINE "AS IT WAS IN THE DAYS OF OLD"

As one journeys through Palestine he is frequently reminded of the truth of the sayings of the Saviour about the shepherd and his sheep.

erence and piety to spots hallowed by religious associations sees the landscapes of the Holy Land through a golden haze that makes them lovely. But the scenery of the Holy Land, taken as a whole (for there are exceptions presently to be noticed), is inferior, both in form and in color, to that of northern and middle Italy, to that of Norway and Scotland, to that of the coasts of Asia Minor, to that of many parts of California and Washington.

The hills are flat-topped ridges, with a monotonous sky-line, very few of them showing any distinctive shape. Not a peak anywhere, and Tabor the only summit recognizable by its form. They are all composed of gray or reddish-gray limestone, bare of wood, and often too stony for tillage. Between the stones or piles of rock there are low shrubs, and in the few weeks of spring masses of brilliant flowers give rich hues to the landscape; but for the rest of the year all is gray or brown. The grass is withered away or is scorched brown, and scarcely any foliage is seen on the tops or upper slopes of the rolling hills. It is only in some of the valleys that one finds villages nestling among olive groves and orchards where plum and peach and almond blossoms make spring lovely.

Arid indeed is the land. The traveler says with the Psalmist: "My soul longs in a dry, parched land, wherein no water is." Wells are few, springs still fewer, and of brooks there are practically none, for the stony channels at the bottom of the glens have no water except after a winter rainstorm. There may probably have been a more copious rainfall 20 or 30 centuries ago, when more wood clothed the hillsides, and the country would then have been more pleasing to Northern eyes, to which mountains are dear because rills make music and green boughs wave in the wind.

THE RIVER KISHON

To this general description there are certain exceptions which must not be forgotten. The high ridge of Mount Carmel rises grandly from the sea, and on its land side breaks down in bold declivities and deep glens upon the valley through which the Kishon, an almost perennial stream, finds its way to the Bay of Acre. Here, upon the slopes of a long ridge, on the other side of the Kishon, there is a wildering forest of ancient holm-oaks, all the more beautiful because it is the one considerable stretch of natural wood in the whole country west of Jordan.

On the other side of that river the slopes of the plateau which runs eastward into the desert, the Bashan and Gilead of the Old Testament, have also patches of woodland left, and in the canyons that cut deep through these slopes there is many a picturesque scene where the brooks, Jabbok and Yarmuk, leap in tiny waterfalls from ledge to ledge of the cliffs. These are the only brooks in all the country, these and the Kishon, which itself is reduced in late summer to a line of pools.

VIEW FROM TABOR

Of the wider views there are two that ought to be noted. One is beautiful. It is the prospect from the top of Mount Tabor, a few miles east of Nazareth, over the wide plain of Esdraelon, specially charming in April, when the green of the upspringing wheat and barley contrasts with the rich red of the strips of newly plowed land that lie between.

The other is grand and solemn. From the Mount of Olives, and indeed from the higher parts of Jerusalem itself, one looks across the deep hollow where the Jordan, a little below

THE VILLAGE WEAVER

In some parts of Palestine the men do the spinning in their spare time, taking the yarn to the village weaver to be converted into cloth, after which the women make it into clothing. European ginghams and calico are rapidly replacing the native product.

Jericho, pours its turbid waters into the Dead Sea, and sees beyond this hollow the long, steep wall of the mountains of Moab.

These mountains are the edge of the great plateau, 3,000 feet higher than the Dead Sea, which extends into the Great Desert of Northern Arabia. Among them is conspicuous the projecting ridge of Nebo, or Pisgah, from which Moses looked out upon that Promised Land which he was not permitted to enter. These mountains are the background of every eastward view from the heights of Judea. Always impressive, they become weirdly beautiful toward sunset, when the level light turns their stern gray to exquisite purples and a tender lilac that deepens into violet as the night begins to fall.

PROSPECTS THAT PLEASE

In eastern Galilee also there are noble prospects of distant Hermon; nor is there any coast scenery anywhere finer than that of the seaward slopes of Lebanon behind Sidon and Beirut. But Hermon and Lebanon (as already remarked) lie outside Palestine and would need a description to themselves. Damascus, seen from the heights above, its glittering white embosomed in orchards, is a marvel of beauty—a pearl set in emeralds, say the Muslims. Petra, far off in the Arabian Desert to the south, is a marvel of wild grandeur, with its deep, dark gorges and towering crags; but these also lie outside Palestine.

THE SEA OF GALILEE

Though not comparable in beauty either to the lakes of Britain or to those that lie among the Alps, or to Lake George in New York and Lake Tahoe in California, the Sea of Galilee has a quiet charm of its own.

The shores are bare of wood and the encircling mountains show no bold peaks: yet the slopes of the hills, sometimes abruptly, sometimes falling in soft and graceful lines, have a pleasing variety, and from several points a glimpse may be caught of the snowy top of Hermon rising beyond the nearer ranges. A great sadness broods over the silent waters. The cities that decked it like a necklace have, all but Tiberias, vanished so utterly that archeologists dispute over their sites. There is little cultivation, and where half a million of people are said to have lived at the beginning of our era, not 5,000 are now to be found. Many a devastating war and the misgovernment of 14 centuries have done their fatal work.

PALESTINE SUMMED UP

If Palestine is not a land of natural wealth nor a land of natural beauty, what is it? What are the impressions which the traveler who tries to see it exactly as it is carries away with him? Roughly summed up, they are these: stones, caves, tombs, ruins, battle-fields, sites hallowed by traditions—all bathed in an atmosphere of legend and marvel.

Never was there a country, not being an absolute desert, so stony. The hillsides seem one mass of loose rocks, larger or smaller. The olive yards and vineyards are full of stones. Even the cornfields (except in the alluvial soil of the plain of Esdraelon and along the sandy coast) seem to have more pebbles than earth, so that one wonders how crops so good as one sometimes sees can spring up. Caves are everywhere, for limestone is the prevailing rock, and it is the rock in which the percolation of rain makes clefts and hollows and caverns most frequent.

ARCHED STREETS OF STEPS: JERUSALEM

Few streets inside the city walls admit of vehicles, and those that do have been remodeled in late years. The slippery pavements are dangerous for shod animals, while the camels, with their cushioned feet, move along with ease. Until a few years ago the streets were unlighted and the law required individuals to carry lanterns after sundown, just as we require automobile lamps to be lighted after dark.

THE ROCKY ROADSTEAD AT JAFFA

At the eastern end of the Mediterranean lies Jaffa, the principal gateway to the Holy Land. Here Cassiopeia, queen of the Ethiopians, according to tradition, boasted herself equal in beauty to the Nereids. The resulting wrath of Poseidon sent a flood and a sea monster, from which no relief could be secured until Cassiopeia's daughter, Andromeda, was chained to the rocks and exposed to the monster. The rock to which she is reputed to have been chained is visible in the picture. From Jaffa, also, Jonah set out on his adventurous voyage (see text, page 69).

HISTORIC CAVES

Many of the incidents of Bible history are associated with caverns, from the cave of Machpelah, at Hebron, where Abraham buried Sarah and in which he is supposed to have been himself interred, down to the sepulchre hewn in rock in which the body of Christ was laid and over which the Church of the Holy Sepulchre was built by Helena, the mother of the Emperor Constantine.

Tradition points out many other sacred caves. It places the Annunciation by the Angel Gabriel to the Virgin at Nazareth in one cavern and the birth of Christ at Bethlehem in another, and assigns others to Samson, to David, to Elijah, and to various prophets. All over the country one finds tombs hewn in the solid rocks and pillars or piles of stone marking a burial place. Many of these rock tombs may be the work of races that dwelt here before Israel came. In a rocky land. where natural cavities are common, this becomes the obvious mode of interment. Thus here, as in Egypt, one seems to be in a land rather of the dead than of the living.

The impression of melancholy which this brooding shadow of death gives is heightened by the abundance of ruins. From very early times men built here in stone because there were, even then, few large trees, and though the dwellings of the poor were mostly of sun-baked mud and have long since vanished, the ease with which the limestone could be quarried and used for building made those who sought defense surround even small towns with walls, whose foundations at least have remained. The larger among the surviving ruins date from Roman or from Crusading times. These are still numerous, though Muslim vandalism and the habit of finding in the old erections material for new

have left comparatively little of architectural interest.

GRECO-ROMAN RUINS

The best preserved remains are those of the Greco-Roman towns east of the Jordan, and these cities, singularly good specimens of the work of their age, are being rapidly destroyed by the Circassians whom the Turks have placed in that region. Be the ruins great or small, they are so numerous that in a course of a day's ride one is everywhere sure to pass far more of them than the traveler could find in even those parts of Europe that have been longest inhabited, and of many the ancient names are lost.

One is amazed at the energy the Crusaders showed in building castles, not a few of them large and all of them solid strongholds, as well as churches. But none of the fortresses are perfect, and of the churches only four or five have been spared sufficiently to show their beauty. Several, among these the most beautiful and best preserved, have been turned into mosques. Of these ruins few are cared for except by the archeologist and the historian.

RELIGIOUS MEMORIALS

But there are other memorials of the past that have lived on into the present. In no country are there so many shrines of ancient worship, so many spots held sacred—some sacred to Jews, some to Christians, some to Mussulmans. Neither has any other country spots that still draw a multitude of pilgrims, not even Belgium and Lombardy, each a profusion of battlefields. It is a land of ancient strife and seldom-interrupted slaughter.

Before Israel came, the tribes of Canaan warred with one another, and against those tribes Israel had to fight for its life. Along its western border ran the great line of march from Egypt to northern Syria and Mesopotamia, the highway of war trodden by the armies of Assyria and Babylon when they passed south to attack Egypt, and by the armies of Egypt when the great Pharaohs, Rameses, Thothmes, and Necho, led them north against Assyria.

In later days the Seleucid kings of Babylon and Antioch had fight after fight for the possession of the country with the Egyptian Ptolemies. Then appeared the legions of Rome, first under Pompey, then many a campaign to quell the revolt of the Jews. Still later came those fiercest enemies of Rome, the Sassanid kings of Persia, whose great invasion of A. D. 614 laid waste Jerusalem and spread ruin over the land.

THE ARAB INVASION

Just after that invasion the Arabs, then in the first flush of their swift conquest, descended on the enfeebled province and set up that Muslim rule which has often changed hands from race to race and dynasty to dynasty, but has never disappeared. When the Mohammedan princes had fought among themselves for four centuries they were suddenly attacked by a host of Crusaders from western Europe, and the soil of Palestine was drenched afresh with blood. The chronicle of more recent wars, which includes Napoleon's irruption, stopped at Acre in 1799, comes down to the Egyptian invasion in the days of Mehemet Ali.

From the top of Mount Tabor one looks down on six famous battlefields—the first, that of the victory of Deborah and Barak over Sisera, Commemorated in the oldest of Hebrew war songs (Judges, Chapters 4-5), and the latest, that of the victory of the French over the Turks in 1799. And in this plain, near the spot where Barak overcame Sisera and Pharaoh Necho overcame Josiah, is to be fought the mysterious Armageddon (Revelation, Chapter 16).

DOMINION OF THE PAST

Caves and tombs, ruins and battlefields, and ancient seats of worship are the visible signs of that dominion of the past, overweighting and almost effacing the present, which one feels constantly and everywhere in Palestine. For us English-speaking men and women, who read the Bible in our youth and followed the *stream* of history down through antiquity and the Middle Ages, no country is so steeped in historical associations.

It could not be otherwise, for in no other country (save Egypt) did history begin so early; none has seen such an unending clash of races and creeds; none has been the theater of so many events touching the mind of so large a part of mankind. The interest which Nature, taken alone, fails to give is given in unequaled profusion by history, and by legend even more than by history.

THE ATMOSPHERE OF LEGEND AND MARVEL

The Holy Land is steeped also in an atmosphere of legend and marvel. As the traveler steps ashore at Jaffa he is shown the rock to which Andromeda was chained when Perseus rescued her from the sea monster. (It is the only Greek story localized on these shores.) Till recent years he was also shown the remains of the ribs of another sea monster, the "great fish" that swallowed and disgorged the prophet Jonah, whose tomb he will see on the coast near Sidon. When he proceeds toward Jerusalem he passes Lydda, the birthplace of St. George,

A SECTION OF THE GREAT MOSAIC MAP OF PALESTINE

In 1880 a Christian settlement was founded about the mound of ancient Madeba. Ten years later the Greek patriarch at Jerusalem heard of a mosaic map at that place and promptly sent a master mason there to preserve it. The mosaic was nearly complete at that time. Instead of preserving it, the mason almost destroyed it, reporting back to Jerusalem that it did not possess the importance which had been attributed to it. In 1897 the librarian of the Greek patriarchate went down to Madeba and found the map one of the greatest archeological discoveries of modern times. It is thought that originally it included all of the country from Constantinople to Egypt. Jerusalem is plainly seen with a colonnaded street running through it, past the Church of the Holy Sepulchre. The Jordan River is shown with fish in it and emptying into the Dead Sea.

where that youthful hero slew the dragon. A little farther comes the spot where another young champion, Samson, the Danite, had in earlier days killed a thousand Philistines with the jaw-bone of an ass.

Still farther along the railway line he is pointed to the opening of the Valley of Ajalon, where, according to the Book of Joshua, the sun and moon stood still while Israel pursued their enemies. An hour later, as the train approaches

THE MARKET-PLACE AT BETHLEHEM

In the Church of the Nativity, at Pethleliem, which stands near the market-place, is the grotto which tradition declares was the manger where Christ was born. Life in Bethlehem has indeed changed but little since His day.

Jerusalem, he looks down on the rocky gorge in which St. Sabas, himself a historical character, famous and influential in the sixth century, dwelt in a cave where a friendly lion came to bear him company; and from Jerusalem he can note the spot at which the host of Israel passed dryshod over Jordan, following the Ark of the Covenant, and near which Elisha made the iron swim and turned bitter waters to sweet. Thence, too, he can descry, far off among the blue hills of Moab, the mountain top to which Balaam was brought to curse Israel, and where "the dumb ass, speaking with man's voice, forbade the mad-ness of the prophet" (Numbers, Chapter 20; 2 Peter, Chapter 1).

WILD MUSLIM LEGENDS

These scenes of marvel, all passing before the eye in a single afternoon, are but a few examples of the beliefs associated with ancient sites over the length and breadth of the country. All sorts of legends have sprung up among Muslims, as well as Jews and Christians, the Muslim legends being indeed the wildest. For nearly every incident mentioned in the Old or New Testament a local site has been found, often one highly improbable, perhaps plainly impossible, which nevertheless the devout are ready to accept.

The process of site-finding had begun before the days of the Empress Helena, and it goes on still. (Quite recently the Muslims have begun to honor a cave at the base of Mount Carmel, which they hold to have sheltered Elijah.) Nothing is more natural, for the number of pilgrims goes on increasing with the increased ease and cheapness of transportation, and sites have to be found for the pilgrims.

CHRISTIAN PILGRIMS

The Roman Catholics come chiefly from France, but they are few compared with the multitude of Russians, nearly all simple peasants, ready to kiss the stones of every spot which they are told that the presence of the Virgin or a saint has hallowed.

To accommodate those pilgrim swarms, for besides the Catholics and the Orthodox, the other ancient churches of the East, such as the Armenians, the Copts, and the Abyssinians, are also represented, countless monasteries and hospices have been erected at and around Jerusalem, Bethlehem, Nazareth, and other sacred spots; and thus the aspect of these places has been so modernized that it is all the more difficult to realize what they were like in ancient days.

Jews have come in large numbers; they have settled in farm colonies; they have built up almost a new quarter on the north side of old Jerusalem. But even they are not so much in evidence as the Christian pilgrims. The pilgrim is now, especially at the times of festival, the dominant feature of Palestine. It is the only country, save Egypt, perhaps even more than Egypt, to which men flock for the sake of the past; and it is here that the philosophic student can best learn to appreciate the part which tradition and marvel have played in molding the minds and stimulating the religious fervor of mankind.

WHAT PALESTINE MIGHT BE

Under a better government—a government which should give honest administration, repress brigandage, diffuse education, irrigate the now desolate, because sun-scorched, valley of the lower Jordan by water drawn from the upper course of the river—Palestine might become a prosperous and even populous country and have its place in the civilization of the present.

The inhabitants, mostly Muslims, are a strong and often handsome race, naturally equal to the races of Southern Europe; but as Palestine stands today, it is a land of the past, a land of memories—memories of religion, but chiefly of religious war, and always rather of war than of peace. The only work ever done in it for peace was done by the preaching, 19 centuries ago, of One whose teaching His followers have never put in practice.

The strife of Israel against the Amorites and of the Crusaders against the Muslims pale to insignificance compared with the conflict between five great nations today who bear the Christian name, and some of whom are claiming the Almighty as their special patron and protector.

To one other kind of impression something remains to be said. Does travel in the Holy Land give a clearer comprehension of the narratives of the Old and New Testament? Does it give a livelier sense of their reality? This question must be answered separately for the two divisions of the Bible.

GALILEE FISHERMEN MENDING THEIR NETS

"A great sadness broods over the silent waters (of Galilee). The cities that decked it like a necklace have, all but Tiberias, vanished so utterly that archaeologists dispute over their sites. There is little cultivation, and where half a million people are said to have lived at the beginning of our era, not 5,000 are now to be found. Many a devastating war and the misgovernment of fourteen centuries have done their fatal work" (see text, page 65).

ISRAEL'S NEIGHBORS

On the Old Testament the traveler gets an abundance of fresh light from visiting the spots it mentions. The history of Israel from the time of Joshua—indeed, from the time of Abraham stands out vividly. One realizes the position of the chosen people in the midst of hostile tribes— some tribes close to them: the Philistines at the western part of the Judean hills; the Tyrians almost within sight of Carmel, to the north; Amalek in the desert to the south, raiding as far as Hebron; Moab and the Beni Ammon on the plateau that lies beyond Jordan to the east, while the Syrian kingdom of Ben-hadad and Hazael threatens from behind the ridges of Galilee.

One sees the track along which the hosts of Egypt and Assyria marched. One feels the breath of the desert upon the prophets, for the desert comes into Palestine itself. One traverses it descending from Jerusalem to the Dead Sea. It lies in bare, brown cliffs above the gardens of Jericho. One understands what the foe of Israel meant when he said that the gods of Israel were gods of the hills, and his own gods of the valleys.

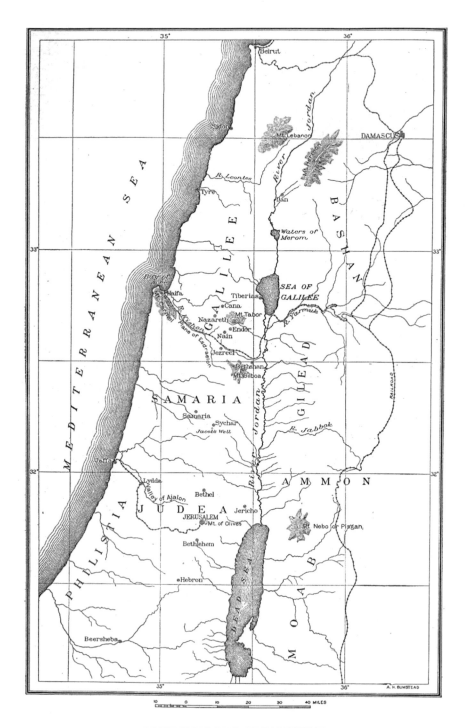

REFERENCE MAP OF PALESTINE

74

HOW NEAR WAS ENDOR!

One sees how near to the Gilboan Mountains was Endor, where Saul went to consult the witch the night before the fatal battle (1 Samuel, Chapter 28), and how near also the wall of Bethshan, to which the Philistines fixed his body and that of the gallant Jonathan. Samaria, the stronghold of Omri, and long afterward of Herod, frowns upon the plain beneath, and at Jezreel the slope is seen up which Jehu drove his steeds so furiously to the slaughter of Jezebel (2 Kings, Chapter 9).

One can feel it all to be real. Elijah runs before the chariot of Ahab while the thunder is pealing above, and Naaman is bathing in Jordan on his way back to Damascus from the visit to Elisha. The historical books of the Old Testament are so full of references to localities that one uses them almost as a handbook. Napoleon, they say, had them read aloud to him in the evenings in his camp on the Syrian expedition of 1799.

And though the aspect of things has been greatly changed since those days by the disappearance of ancient forests, the introduction of some new trees and new kinds of buildings, not to speak of two railways and a few macadamized roads, still the natural features of hill and valley remain, and there is much in the ways and customs of the people that remains the same. The shepherd leads the same life, except that he has no longer to fear the lion, who has long since vanished, nor the bear, who survives only in the recesses of the northern hills.

NEW TESTAMENT PALESTINE

When one turns to the New Testament, how great is the difference. Except as regards Jerusalem and the Sea of Galilee, there are scarcely any references to localities in the Gospel narratives, and in those few references little or nothing turns upon the features of the place.

We can identify some of the spots where miracles are related, such as Nain and Cana of Galilee, but the events are not connected with any special feature of the locality. Journeys are mentioned, but not the route along which Christ passed, except Sychar, in the Samaritan territory, where was Jacob's well, one of the few sacred spots which can be positively identified. (The Crusaders erected a church over it which is now being restored by Franciscan monks.) The cities round the Sea of Galilee have, all except Tiberias, vanished from the earth, and the sites of most of them are doubtful.

The town now called Nazareth has been accepted for many centuries as the home of Christ's parents, but the evidence to prove it so is by no means clear, and it is hard to identify the cliff on which the city was built. The Mount of Olives, in particular, and the height on its slope, where Christ, following the path from Bethany, looked down on Jerusalem, and the temple in all its beauty, are the spots at which one seems to get into the closest touch with the Gospel narrative; and it is just here that the scene has been most changed by new buildings, high walls, villas and convents and chapels. Even the scenic conditions and whatever we may call "the setting" of the parables belong rather to the eastern world than to Palestine. You do not feel the incidents to be the more real because they are placed in this particular part of the East.

THE ACTUAL AND THE IDEAL

All this makes the traveler realize afresh and from a new side that while the Old Testament

EASTER WEEK AT THE RIVER JORDAN

Next to a pilgrimage to Jerusalem, the water from the River Jordan is one of the greatest things the deeply religious peasants of Russia, Greece, Bulgaria, and Turkey wish for. Thousands of devoted pilgrims come to this holy river in order to bathe in the stream, that they may be washed of their sin. Every pilgrim to the River Jordan fills a bottle with the sacred water to take home, so that those who cannot make the journey may avail themselves of its purifying powers.

is about and for Israel, as well as composed in the land of Israel, the Gospel, though their narrative is placed in the land and the preaching was delivered to the people of Israel, is addressed to the world.

The Old Testament books, or at least the legal and historical books, are concerned with one people, with the words and deeds of its kings and prophets and warriors, whereas the New Testament is concerned with the inner life of all mankind. The one is of the concrete, the other of the abstract; the one of the actual, the

other of the ideal. The actual is rooted in time and place; the ideal is independent of both. It is only in parts of the poetical and prophetic books that the teaching becomes ideal and universal, like that of the New Testament.

It ought perhaps to be added that the incidents of Chronicles in the Old Testament belong (except, of course, when the element of marvel comes in) to what may be called normal history, and can therefore be realized just as easily as we realize the wars of the Crusaders and the deeds of Sultan Saladin.

A VIEW OF THE HOLY CITY, WITH THE MOUNT OF OLIVES IN THE BACKGROUND

The population of Jerusalem has been estimated at 60,000. The Muslims number about 7,000, the Jews 40,000, and the Christians 13,000. The Muslims are the rulers and at the head of the social scale—the aristocracy of the city—since Saladin reconquered it in the year 1187.

THE GOSPEL AND PALESTINE

We picture to ourselves the battle of Saul and the Philistines at Gilboa as we picture the battle of Napoleon against the Turks, a few miles farther north. It is much harder to fit the Gospel with the framework of Jerusalem or Galilee, because its contents are unlike anything else in history. An Indian Mussulman scholar or a thoughtful Buddhist from Japan might not feel this, but it is hard for a European or American Christian not to feel it.

Whether these explanations be true or not, it is the fact that to some travelers the sight of the places that are mentioned in the Gospel seems to bring no further comprehension of its meaning, no heightened emotion, except that which the thought that they are looking upon the very hills, perhaps treading the very paths that were trodden by the feet of Christ and the Apostles, naturally arouses. The narrative remains to them in just the same ideal, non-local atmosphere which surrounded it in their childhood. It still belongs to the realm of the abstract, to the world of the soul rather than to the world of physical nature. It is robed not in the noonday glare of Palestine,

THE SUPPOSED POINT OF THE CROSSING OF THE JORDAN
BY THE CHILDREN OF ISRAEL

Religion, history, and nature conspire to make the Jordan the most famous river of the earth. Across it the hosts of Israel were led into the Promised Land; in its waters the Christian right of baptism had its birth; up and down its valley many civilizations in the morning of history rose and fell. Perhaps the strangest thing about this famous river is that none of the ancients ever guessed that its mouth was below the level of the sea. It was not until 1874 that accurate measurements were made and the mouth of the river was found 1,292 feet below the Mediterranean, less than sixty miles away.

as they see it today, nor even in the rich purple which her sunsets shed upon the far-off hills, but in a celestial light that never was on sea or land.

TYPICAL PILGRIM'S VIEWPOINT

These persons, however, mostly Protestants, are the few exceptions. The typical pilgrim, be he or she a Roman Catholic Legitimist from France or an unlettered peasant from Russia, accepts everything and is edified by everything. The Virgin and the saints have always been so real to these devout persons, the sense of their reality heightened by constant prayers before the Catholic image or the Russian icon, that it is natural for the pilgrim to think of them as dwelling in the very spots which the guide points out, and the marvelous parts of the legends present to them no difficulty.

The French Catholic has probably been on a pilgrimage to Lourdes and drawn health from the holy spring in its sacred cavern. The Russian peasant has near his home some wonder-working picture. The world to him is still full of religious miracles, and Palestine is but the land in which the figures who consecrate the spots are the most sacred of all those whom Christianity knows. To him to die in it is happiness, for death is the portal to Heaven. Nowhere else does one see a faith so touching in its simplicity.

A ROMANTIC JOURNEY

To all travelers who have anything of poetry in their hearts, be they pilgrims or tourists, or critical archeologists and historians, there is, and there will always be, an inexpressible romance in this journey. Palestine is preëminently the Land of the Past—a land whose very air is charged with the human emotions and the memories of human action, reaching far back into the dim twilight of prehistoric centuries.

No one who is in any degree susceptible to the impressions of nature or of history can help feeling the glamour of the country. The colors of distant hills, seen at morn or even through this clear, keen air, seem rich and sad with pathos of ages of human effort and human passion. The imagination is always trying to body forth the men and women who lived beneath these skies, the heroes of war and the saints of suffering, the nameless poets, and the prophets who live on in their burning words, and to give them visible form and life.

Imagination always fails, but it never desists from the attempt, and though it cannot visualize the scenes, it feels the constant presence of these shadowy figures. In them, shadowy as they are, in the twilight of far-off ages, the primal forces of humanity were embodied—in them its passionate aspirations seem to have their earliest, simplest, and most moving expression.

THE LAST ISRAELITISH BLOOD SACRIFICE

How the Vanishing Samaritans Celebrate the Passover on Sacred Mount Gerizim

By John D. Whiting

Author of "From Jerusalem to Aleppo," "Village Life in the Holy Land,"
and "Jerusalem's Locust Plague," in the National Geographic Magazine

*Illustrated with the only set of night photographs ever taken of this ancient ceremony,
and numerous other unique pictures, by the American Colony Photographers, Jerusalem, Palestine*

SHECHEM, Samaria, and Neapolis were once great cities of the ancient civilized world. Today their glory and importance are no more, save in history. Here alone we find a dying and almost extinct community of Samaritans, the remnant of a once numerous sect, whose persistent continuation and literal performance of the Passover Sacrifice have attracted the attention of students for more than three centuries.

Nablus, the modern Shechem, the only home of the Samaritans of today, is a town of about 27,000 inhabitants, lying some forty miles north of Jerusalem. The population is chiefly Moslem, the remainder being composed of various Christian sects, together with a mere handful of Samaritans. But as yet no Jew has settled there, the Biblical axiom still holding good, "for the Jews have no dealings with the Samaritans."

Besides being a center of trade, Nablus has gained a little fame for its soap, made of pure olive oil, a variety which, though crudely manufactured, is used almost exclusively by the people of the city, and is much prized by the natives of Syria and Egypt.

NABLUS (THE MODERN SHECHEM),
THE ONLY HOME OF THE SAMARITANS TODAY

The town nestles in the valley which lies between Mount Ebal and Mount Gerizim. The picture is taken from the lower slopes of Gerizim, near Ras el Ain, while Mount Ebal is seen in the background (see map, page 104).

The town nests in a confined valley running east and west, between twin mountains—Ebal, some 3,000 feet above sea-level, which looms up on the north, and the lesser Gerizim, about 150 feet lower, which closes in on the south, with its base in places only a few hundred yards from that of its mate.

From the lower slopes of Gerizim issue numerous and copious springs. The modern town has therefore crept up in their direction. These waters, after filling the demand made upon them by the city, find their way into extensive gardens to the west, where flourish fig trees, laden with delicious fruit, pomegranates hung with scarlet bloom and fruit, yellow quinces, walnuts, mulberries, olives, and occasional bitter-orange trees raised for the perfume extracted from the flowers. Among the trees many varieties of vegetables grow in abundance.

The houses of the town are dome-roofed and lattice-windowed, constructed from the soft, white limestone of Mount Ebal. The streets are picturesquely narrow and most of them are paved with cobble-stones, with here and there an arch thrown across and supporting a room above.

THE HOME CITY OF THE SAMARITANS

In the "souks," or markets, as in most Syrian towns, the stores are so small that the customer stands outside to examine the meager display of European and native (Damascene) wares. Here are rows of silversmith shops, where the artisans work cross-legged, producing from crude silver elaborate ornaments for the peasant women. Here are the coffee shops, the street in front blockaded with men sitting upon low stools, sipping the thick, hot beverage from tiny cups and smoking the long, red-piped, bub-

bling narghile as they gossip and play a game of "tawla."

Next are the sweetmeat venders, from whose stalls large trays of "kanafie" protrude into the street. This pastry dish, for which Nablus is noted, has a filling of fresh, sweet cheese. After it is baked, melted butter and thick syrup are poured over it until it is literally soaked with the mixture.

From the chief market-place the Samaritan Quarter of Nablus is approached from the north through long, tunnel-like lanes which lead to the very foot of the sacred mountain.

Just above the city, Gerizim is steep and rocky, and the trees disappear. In summer the mountain side is gray and barren, but in winter even the smallest patches of earth are scratched with primitive plows and sown with wheat or barley.

THE FRIENDLY CACTUS

Across from the town the slopes of Ebal present a very different picture. Equally rocky, they are still perennially green with cactus bushes planted among the rock ledges, which are curiously studded with ancient sepulchers, whose open doors from a distance reveal only the darkness within. Some of these tombs were rifled centuries ago; others have come to light within the past few years. Many have stone doors and stone hinges, with stone locks still in working condition if the keys, probably of bronze, could be found.

But the modern inhabitants do not pride themselves on this interesting cemetery, as did the peoples of bygone times. To the Arabs of today antique relics are of no import; but they feel justly proud of the cactus or prickly-pear bushes, which present a weird spectacle and cover every available space in this oriental

THE HILL OF SAMARIA

Omri, the sixth king of Israel, in the ninth century B. C., bought an isolated hill a few miles west of Shechem, where he built his capital and named it Samaria, after its original owner.

THE ACROPOLIS OF SAMARIA

The city of Samaria from its inception overshadowed its rival, Shechem, and perhaps under Roman rule attained the pinnacle of its glory. The Emperor Augustus presented it to Herod the Great, who rebuilt and embellished it after the Roman style and renamed it Sebaste.

God's Acre. The fame of these bushes reaches as far as the Bosporus, where the much-prized fruit is a favorite gift among the notables of Constantinople.

The prickly-pear cactus was first introduced into Palestine by the Crusaders; today it is grown throughout the length and breadth of the land, being valuable not only for its fruit,

REBURYING AHAB'S PALACE: SAMARIA

The enormous quantity of earth removed by the American excavators in clearing these ruins was conveyed in baskets on the heads of women, who, like ants, formed an endless chain of toil, running back and forth. Once the archeological researches had been made, the ruins were again filled with the dust of remote ages, thus preserving them for future generations as well as returning the land to its owners in its original state.

but also as an excellent hedge. The natives, however, do not yet appreciate its great value as forage for cattle. The camels help themselves to it whenever they get a chance, their mouths being so tough that, regardless of the spines, they devour the leaves with unmistakable relish. The Ebal cactus' superiority lies in the extra large size of its fruit, the tenderness of its seeds, and its sweet and luscious flavor, due both to the peculiar soil and to the protection afforded from the cold north winds. The Arabic name for the pear, *sobbir* (patience), seems eminently appropriate to one who has innocently handled the unpeeled fruit and had

his hands filled with the microscopic spines, which can be extracted only by painful laboriousness.

SHECHEM, WHERE THE BIBLE INTRODUCES ABRAHAM

The first city built in this valley was Shechem, which occupied a site a short distance to the east of Nablus. Here, at the highest point of the valley, where the rains to the east find their way to the Dead Sea and those to the west to the Mediterranean, is a small artificial hill. Recent excavations by archeologists have revealed a city wall encircling the remains

SAMARITAN GIRLS LEARNING THEIR ANCIENT HEBREW

Note the latticed windows, used so extensively in the East to prevent men in the neighborhood from looking into the women's apartments.

of houses and have laid bare numerous ancient earthenware vessels.

As we look upon these primitive habitations, more than 3,000 years old, it is hard to realize that we are not actually looking on the oldest city built here, but upon a town that, at this early date, had already had a long existence.

It is at Shechem, then called "Sichem," and the plain of Moreh, into which the Shechem gorge opens at its eastern extremity, that Biblical history introduces Abraham, the father of the Hebrews, in Canaan. Likewise Jacob made this locality his first halt on returning from his sojourn with Laban in Haran. Here he purchased the parcel of ground whither, at a later date, Joseph's bones were brought from Egypt to be buried, and where today Jacob's well is pointed out as the spot at which Jesus and the Samaritan woman met (see map, page 104).

Immediately following the Israelitish invasion of Canaan and the taking of Jericho and Ai, Joshua built upon Ebal the first altar of sacrifice erected by his people in the new land.

The Shechem Valley now became the theater of the first general convocation, and, according to the Mosaic injunction, the whole congregation was assembled, "half of them over against Mount Gerizim and half of them over against Mount Ebal." From Ebal were to be

THE SAMARITAN SYNAGOGUE

This, the only house of worship which the Samaritans possess, is a very plain building and only a few hundred years old. In the recess to the left, behind ornamented curtains, are primitive safes and cupboards containing many parchments and Pentateuchs, among them the noted Abishua Codex (see illustration, page 92).

ONE OF THE SYNAGOGUE CURTAINS

This silken curtain, heavily embroidered in gold, is used in the synagogue to hang in front of the scroll chests. The designs represent the cup of manna, ark of the covenant, Aaron's rod blossoming, the seven-branched candlestick, the table of shew-bread, the golden censer, and other temple furnishings such as existed in the temple at Jerusalem.

proclaimed the curses against those who should forsake the law of their God, and from Gerizim the blessings that would result in the following of *Yahweh* (the unpronounced Hebrew name for God).

Here also, just before his death, Joshua addressed the last assembly of the people, making a covenant with them.

We now come to the broader period of its history. Ephraim, destined to figure as the leading tribe of the Northern Kingdom, had the lot of its possession fall to the district wherein Shechem lay. This territory was then known as "Mount Ephraim."

The town of Shechem itself was apportioned to the Levites, since they, being a tribe of priests, received no inheritance except cities and their suburbs in which to dwell throughout all the tribes. Shechem was also selected as one of the cities of refuge, and throughout the Hebraic occupation held an important place.

During the period of the Judges little of importance is heard of Mount Ephraim, except that Abimelech, son of Gideon by a Shechemite concubine, was made "King" of Shechem, and ruled three years.

With the advent of David came the Golden Age of the Hebrews. The capital was moved to Jerusalem, where, upon his succession, Solomon built the renowned Temple and established thereby a center of worship.

But this unified kingdom was short-lived, and with the death of Solomon, his son, Rehoboam, proceeded to Shechem, where all Israel was gathered to make him king. Instead of this being consummated, ten tribes revolted and made Jeroboam, an attache of Solomon's court, king. Jeroboam selected Shechem as his home. Thus the northern ten tribes established the

Kingdom of Israel, now forever rent from the Kingdom of Judah, which was composed of the two remaining tribes, Judah and Benjamin.

Omri, the sixth king of Israel, in the ninth century B. C., bought an isolated hill a few miles west of Shechem, on the north side of the valley, and there built his capital, naming it Samaria, after its original owner. At the time of the First Captivity the Kingdom of Israel lost its northernmost tribes and its possessions beyond the Jordan. From them Galilee was then created, while the remaining southern part inherited the name of its once important capital, Samaria, and became a State subject to Assyria. Thus was the land cut up into three districts— Galilee, Samaria, and Judea.

SEBASTE, CITY OF HEROD

The city of Samaria, from its inception, overshadowed its rival, Shechem, and probably attained the height of its glory under Roman rule; for the Emperor Augustus presented it to his procurator, Herod the Great, who rebuilt and embellished it after the Roman style, and renamed it Sebaste (Greek for Augusta). Much of Herod's work still remains, notably a double colonnade encircling the hill's crest.

An Arab proverb says, "Beyond every mountain ascent there is a descent." And Sebaste, after climbing to the zenith of power, slowly relapsed into insignificance; so that today, amid the ruins of its splendid past, a squalid mud village bears the once grand title (the name in Arabic being slightly altered to "Sehastieh"). Here is a rare instance, possibly the only one in Palestine, where the Greek name has outlived the older Semitic form.

Sebaste had become a place of no importance more than four centuries before the Emperor Vespasian founded Neapolis (New City)

A VIEW OF MODERN SEBASTE AND THE SURROUNDING HILLS

After climbing to the zenith of might, Sebaste slowly relapsed into insignificance. Today, amid the ruins of a splendid past, a squalid mud village occupies the site and retains the name.

in the Shechem vale, west of the older town, in 67 A. D. This "New City" soon outstripped the older Shechem, and in the fourth century became one of the foremost cities of Palestine—a distinction which it still enjoys under its Arabic name of Nablus.

ABU EL HASSAN,
SON OF THE LATE HIGH PRIEST JACOB

All the Samaritan priests wear long hair, which they wind under their dome-shaped fezzes. "And the Lord said unto Moses, speak unto the priests and say unto them that they shall not make baldness upon their beads; nor shall they shave off the corner of their beards" (Lev. 21: 1-5).

The Samaritan religion is closely akin to that of the Jews, the chief differences being that the cult of the former centers about Gerizim, while that of the Jews centers about Zion, and that the Samaritan canon of Scripture is restricted to the Pentateuch, or "Five Books of Moses." The later writings, including the Prophets and Psalms, the Samaritans repudiate as uninspired.

In view of the similarity in their beliefs and practices, it seems strange that there exists and always has existed the fiercest animosity between Jew and Samaritan, but it is the animosity that invariably exists between an original and a schism.

The Samaritans maintain that they are the remnants and descendants of the once great tribe of Ephraim, and that the split between them and the Jews came about through the mal-administration of the priesthood by Eli's sons. Followers of the Jewish Church are looked upon as dissenters from the pure faith of Israel, and the forming of a center of worship in Jerusalem by Judah is condemned upon the ground that the land of Ephraim, with Shechem and its mountains, figured in the earliest history of the Hebrews; that here the first Israelitish altars were erected, and that these were the only specific parts of the Land of Promise mentioned by Moses in the wilderness.

THE RENOWNED SAMARITAN SCROLL PHOTOGRAPHED AT LAST

The most precious document of this sect is the renowned Samaritan scroll Pentateuch. This scroll is some seventy feet long, and toward the end its columns are divided vertically by a small gap, often occurring between the letters of the same word. Into this gap is carried and written any letter that occurs in the lines

THE FIRST PHOTOGRAPH EVER TAKEN OF THE ABISHUA CODEX,
PROBABLY THE OLDEST COPY OF THE FIRST FIVE BOOKS OF THE BIBLE IN EXISTENCE

The date inscription on the scroll presents to the Samaritan mind indisputable proof that it was written by the great-grandson of Aaron in the early years of the entrance of Israel into Canaan. This Scroll of Abishua, as it is known, has now for the first time been photographed from end to end and will be published in exact life size. It is hoped that when these photographic copies are available to Hebrew students new light may be thrown upon many Scriptural controversies.

which fits into the writing of the date, so that when reading the text it fills its place, while on the other hand these separated letters when read collectively from the top of the column to the bottom, like the Chinese, spell out the name and date of the writer, etc., thus making it impossible for the date to have been of a later writing than that of the scroll itself.

The Samaritans assert that the scroll was written by Abishua, the great-grandson of Aaron, in the early years of the entrance into Canaan, but no impartial student will allow it

this very remote origin, although it is believed to be the most ancient copy of the Pentateuch in existence.

So jealously guarded is this scroll that few non-Samaritans have ever seen it, and many of the Samaritans themselves have not seen it except as it is exhibited on rare occasions at feasts, rolled up and covered with a silken cloth and with but one column exposed.

The scroll has recently been photographed from end to end, and will soon be published for the benefit of Hebrew scholars.

JACOB, SON OF AARON, LATE SAMARITAN HIGH PRIEST

Members of the present priestly family trace their ancestry to the tribe of Levi. The direct Aaronic line that existed till modern times has now failed.

A YOUNG PRIEST WRITING A SAMARITAN PENTATEUCH

All the Samaritan Pentateuchs and prayer books, as well as the books used by the school children, are hand-written. Parchment was used up to two centuries ago; since then paper has come into vogue. Aside from the fact that the poverty of the modern Samaritan commends the use of paper, which is much cheaper, the orthodox scholar will not write on leather unless the hide from which it is prepared has been taken from an animal slaughtered by a priest.

THE VILLAGE OF ASKAR, ANCIENT SYCHAR

Just behind the village is Jacob's well. The mountain in the background is Gerizim, while the mosque on its summit marks the site of the Samaritan temple to which, no doubt, the Samaritan woman pointed when conversing with Jesus.

It is, of course, impracticable to display this very fragile parchment continually, but it is unfortunate that the modern Samaritans impose upon their guests by showing them a scroll of much later date than the one which all so covet to see. The imposition has gone further, for all

photographs made heretofore supposedly of the original Abishua scroll, as it is called, have in reality been of the later copy.

While the Jews have scattered all over the world since the captivities and have absorbed much that is foreign, in many instances adapt-

NEAR SYCHAR IS JACOB'S WELL;
ITS DEPTH IS INDICATED BY THE LENGTH OF THE ROPE

To the east, towering above the encampment, is the loftiest of Gerizim's peaks, crowned with ruins—a spot where once temples stood.

LAMBS SELECTED FOR THE SACRIFICE OF THE PASSOVER

ing their religious practices to their new environment, the Samaritans have during the same lapse of time lived in the land of their forefathers, among Semitic peoples akin to the Hebrews, and because of this fact have handed down to the twentieth century a glimpse of the old Jewish Church almost in its purity. A notable instance of the survival of an ancient religious ceremony is the celebration of the Passover Sacrifice.

One of the distinctive differences between the Samaritan and the Jew lies in their methods of computing the calendar. Instead of adopting the lunar year solely, the Samaritans base their calculations on the moon but they are at the same time also governed by the movement of the sun. The system is so complicated as to form one of the chief studies of the young priests. Basing their authority on the first chapter of Genesis for thus differentiating from the Hebrew calendar, they point out that, in the history of creation, when the sun and moon are introduced, it is said of them jointly, "Let them be for signs, and for seasons, and for days and years" (Gen. 1:14). For the above reasons the Samaritans some years celebrate their Passover with, or nearly with, the Jews, while at other times their fourteenth of Abib comes a month behind.

PREPARING FOR
THE FEAST OF THE PASSOVER

A few days before the Passover the Samaritan ghetto becomes the scene of much activity. Mules and donkeys are loaded with tents and other necessities, while young and old, sick and well, quit their homes to make the pilgrimage to Gerizim, in obedience to the command, "Thou mayest not sacrifice the Passover within any of thine own gates, but in the place which Yahweh thy God shall choose to make a habitation for His name." Often, persons seriously ill are carried in their sick beds to the camp, and here not infrequently babes are born.

Prior to the date appointed, much time is spent in arranging the camp, rebuilding the *tanoor*, or ground oven, used in roasting the sacrifice, and in procuring the necessary wood and brush for fuel.

The ascent to the camp spot on Gerizim requires usually an hour, whether mounted or on foot. Nablus is left behind by a path leading up from its western suburbs, and passing the

THE CONGREGATION GATHERING FOR THE SACRIFICIAL CEREMONY

As they assemble one by one they spread small prayer cloths upon the ground. Upon these they stand with bare feet, having dropped their prayer slippers behind them.

THE ANCIENT HEBREW PRAYER POSTURE SURVIVES TODAY
ON MOUNT GERIZIM

So reverent were the ancient Hebrews that the name of their God never was pronounced publicly, a fact which gave rise to the "coined word," Jehovah, by which the God of the Old Testament Israel now is known. The proper term was "Yahweh." When this word occurred in Hebrew texts another name, "Adonay," was substituted by the priest, and to warn the reader against pronouncing the Holy "Yahweh" the substitute word frequently was printed under the true name. When the Christian translators of the Middle Ages undertook to make the Bible intelligible to the peoples of Europe they apparently did not know what to make of this double term, so they combined the consonants of "Yahweh" with the vowels of "Adonay" to form the "Jehovah" of the King James version.

Samaritan cemetery, an open field, its rocky and stone-strewn surface overgrown with weeds on which donkeys and cattle may be seen browsing. The trail leads up in short, stiff, winding courses through a slight depression where olives and other trees grow vigorously. The way soon becomes so steep that beasts as well as pedestrians are forced to halt at intervals for breath. But the time is not wasted, for the view of the town in its glaring whiteness below,

fringed with verdant gardens and nestling between the twin mountains, is a scene truly beautiful.

THE ENCAMPMENT
OF THE ISRAELITES

Once up this steep ascent, the ridge is gained. Along it the path, now fairly level, leads to a slight depression in the saddle, where suddenly the visitor sees before him more than forty

THE SAMARITAN PASSOVER CAMP,
THE ONLY REMAINING ISRAELITISH CAMP IN THE WORLD

To the east, towering above the encampment, is the loftiest of Gerizim's peaks, crowned with ruins—a spot where once temples stood.

THE TRENCH-ALTAR PREPARED FOR THE SAMARITAN PASSOVER

Two large copper kettles filled with water are placed over this altar. At a short distance, and higher than the altar level, is the *tanoor*, or ground oven, for the sheep-roasting. The men in the right background are tending the oven.

white Egyptian and Damascus tents, the only veritable Israelitish encampment of religious significance in the world.

A pity it is that these more modern tents are used instead of the primitive goat-hair ones of the Bedouins, which would more nearly, if not entirely, resemble those used during the Exodus.

To the east, towering above the encampment, is the loftiest of Gerizim's peaks, crowned with ruins, a spot where once temples stood.

It is Passover eve. Selected sacrificial lambs are contentedly wandering about, unconscious of their impending fate. They have been purchased some days in advance of the Passover, in obedience to the law, "in the tenth day of this month they shall take to them every man a lamb. . . . Your lamb shall be without blemish, a male of the first year. . . . And ye shall keep it up until the fourteenth day of the same month."

But the scene is not quiet. Scores of people, non-Samaritan, young and old, have come up to "smell the air," for to the Nablus people, and especially for the lads, it is a day of excitement not to be missed.

The camp ground is a small, elongated field, the property of the Samaritans. No special system is observed in pitching the tents, beyond leaving a path between the two uneven rows. Each family has one tent; a few have two.

At the eastern extremity of the camp is the *kiniseh* (synagogue), where the religious rites are observed while in camp. It is a small, oblong plot surrounded by a low rubble wall except to the east, where terrace above terrace, now much dilapidated, rises in step form to the mountain crest beyond.

THE TRENCH-ALTAR

At the northern end of this space, or prayer inclosure, a trench has been dug and lined with uncut stone. "An altar of earth shalt thou make unto me. . . . And if thou wilt make an altar of stone, thou shalt not build it of hewn stone; for if thou lift up thy tool upon it, thou hast polluted it."

Across this altar two large copper kettles, filled with water, are placed. Beyond the northeastern end of the inclosure, and higher than its level, is the *tanoor*, or ground oven, for the sheep-roasting. It is a pit, the depth equal to a man's height, from five to six spans in diameter, and lined in a circular form, like a well, with rough stones. Here the rock crops out so near the surface that, in order to get the *tanoor* deep enough, it has to be built partly above the surface and a terrace filled in about it, thus of necessity elevating it above the rest of the space devoted to the Passover observances.

It is about three hours before dark as we arrive, and since the Samaritan time starts its count from sunset, let us forget our Western watches while we remain on Gerizim's heights.

On approaching the camp, one of the first things to attract our attention is the cloud of smoke pouring forth from the *tanoor* and curling skyward from beneath the kettles, for five hours of steady heat produced by burning "saris" brush and thorn bushes are required before the oven is ready for fleecing the sheep.

To escape the confusion caused by the swarms of sight-seers, boys galloping about on their horses or urging on lazy donkeys, hawkers calling out in loud voices as they peddle small cakes, oranges, or sweetmeats, we follow a friend, one of the priests, up to the crest of Gerizim. This, to the Samaritan, is the holiest part of the earth and crowded with sacred spots and associations.

THE SACRED SITES OF GERIZIM

Here one is shown the place where Joshua built the first altar of sacrifice with twelve stones taken from the Jordan. Just above it are the foundations of St. Mary's Church, built by the Emperor Zeno and restored by Justinian. Adjoining these ruins is a small domed mosque, Sheik Ghanim, now in a neglected condition. A Moslem shrine and a Christian church each in succession built on the site from materials supplied by the remains of a Roman temple!

Proceeding southward along the outmost ledge of the plateau, the priests point to spots where tradition says the altars of Adam and of Noah stood. Below is the path by which Adam was expelled from Paradise, after having been created from the dust of Gerizim.

Beyond is the altar of Seth, a stone circle with a pavement of large uncut stones (probably of megalithic origin).

COLLECTING FOR EVENING PRAYERS ON GERIZIM

Before all prayers the Samaritan observes prescribed ablutions, almost identical with the present customs of the Moslems, and like them he now spreads his prayer cloth.

Just beyond Seth's shrine, farther south, is a ditch sunk into a rock protruding boldly from the mountain side. It is the Samaritan rival to Mount Moriah, in Jerusalem. Here the Samaritans believe that Abraham prepared to offer up in sacrifice his only son, and just behind is the

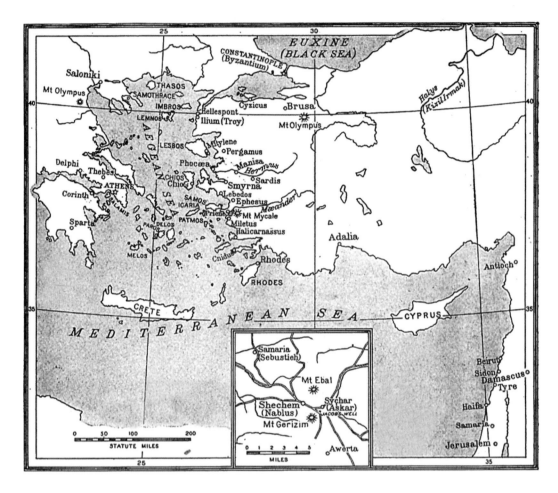

A MAP OF ASIA MINOR AND THE HOLY LAND

Showing the home cities of the Seven Wise Men of ancient Greece and the land of the Samaritans. (Note, in the small inset map, the relative location of Mount Gerizim and Mount Ebal and the historic cities, ancient and modern, which have clung to their slopes—see text, pages 80-89).

place where the ram was found caught in the thicket.

Almost at our feet, far below, in the plain of Askar (Sychar), lay Jacob's well, concealed beneath an uncompleted church erected upon Crusader foundations. Under the spell of the hour and the scene, one could almost picture the Samaritan woman pointing to Gerizim and saying to Jesus, "Our fathers worshiped in *this* mountain, and ye say that in Jerusalem is the place where men ought to worship" (John 4:20).

THE SAMARITAN HOLY OF HOLIES

In the center of the plateau is a large flat rock which the Samaritans call "Kuds el Akdas"; for, according to their tradition, it formed the Holy of Holies of their temple. They approach it only on certain festal occasions and with bared feet. This rock at once calls to memory the rival Rock Moriah lying beneath the gorgeous Dome of the Rock in Jerusalem.

Although less extensive than that from its taller mate, Mt. Ebal, which cuts off the distant Galilee view northward, the scene from Gerizim is broad and grand. In the spring the Plain of Moreh, or Sychar, just at its feet, is a patchwork of small fields in different stages of growth. Near the village of Askar (Sychar), watered from a copious spring, large patches of onions and garlic flourish, their green varying with that of the waving barley and wheat beyond and contrasting with the bare and rocky surrounding hills. The elevations are dotted with villages, and among them, to the southward, is Awerta, where, under the shade of a great tree, the tombs of Aaron's son and grandson, Eleazer and Phinehas, lie.

Directly to the east, separated from the foreground by the deep Jordan chasm, rise the Mountains of Gilead. Like Moab, of which they are a continuation northward, they are suffused with a mysterious and fascinating translucent blue, resembling some precious stone, and never cease to captivate the vision, especially upon clear days. The highest peak, Jebel Osha, crowned by the reputed tomb of Hosea, stands out conspicuously. Towering at the head of the Jordan Valley, Hermon, with its perennial snow-cap, closes the northern limit of this eastern view.

At the foot of Mt. Ebal and bordering upon the plain directly below us are the excavations of ancient Shechem. Near them a small white dome marks the traditional site of the tomb of Joseph. Southward the view stretches over the long mountain range which is the backbone of Palestine, rising between the Phoenician plain and the deep Jordan chasm. When viewed from the Mediterranean, the only break seen in the range is this Valley of Nablus, while its rivals in historic importance, Jerusalem and Hebron, are hidden from view. Mizpah is easily visible, but no glimpse of Jerusalem save a little of its suburbs under favorable conditions.

Turning westward, the mountains and hill country, dotted with villages, drop off gently into a plain which extends to the blue Mediterranean. The ruins of Caesarea, which under Roman rule became the most important city and seaport in Palestine, and often connected with the history of the Apostles and the early Church, are visible under favorable conditions; also the orange groves of Jaffa.

Now the sun is soon setting, and we shall have to hurry back to camp if we are to see all the service which commemorates the Exodus from Egypt.

PRAYER POSTURE AND ROBES SIMILAR TO MOSLEMS

As we descend, white-robed figures are seen collecting about the smoking trench-altar. As they slowly gather one by one they spread on the ground small prayer cloths, upon which they stand with bare feet, having discarded their prayer slippers.

While witnessing this ceremony we were impressed by the striking resemblance to the Moslem garb and posture during prayer. The clothing of the Samaritan on this occasion is, in the main, white, the outside garment being a

THE SAMARITAN HIGH PRIEST JACOB LEADING THE PASSOVER SERVICE

Note the prayer cloth on which he stands. Some of these have the prayer-niche design identical with those of the Moslems. The Samaritans always face their Holy of Holies (the holy rock on the crest of Mount Gerizim) when worshiping.

jubbie made of muslin, identical in cut with that worn by Mohammedan religious sheiks and by the old-style city Moslems, who happily are not adopting western ideas and modes of clothing. Around a dome-shaped fez the priest winds a white turban, sometimes embroidered in amber silk.

The older men of the laity use the same turban, with the customary flat-topped fez, while the young men and boys, like the Mohammedan youths, wear no turbans and are usually clad in white shirts and drawers. The Samaritans, except when in prayer, wear deep wine-colored turbans, as the result of an edict of one of the caliphs, to distinguish them from their Mohammedan neighbors, for originally they wore white and were often mistaken for Moslem sheiks learned in the Koran. Similarly, the Jews formerly used black as a distinguishing hue.

Before all prayers, the Samaritan goes through prescribed ablutions, washing with water three times each the hands, mouth, nose, face, ears, and feet, in this order, and, like the Moslem, he spreads the prayer cloth, which in some instances has the *mihrab* design.

FACING THE HOLY OF HOLIES

Now all have congregated. The venerable high priest, Yakoub (Jacob), feeble and infirm, clad in a pale-green *jubbie*, takes his place in front of the congregation. The two second priests, Ishak (Isaac) and Tewfik, stand slightly behind the high priest. Then come in rows the elders according to rank. Now all the males of the community are present, the smallest boys lining up at right angles to the foremost ranks.

On every hand the walls and terraces are jammed with onlookers, mostly boys and youths of Nablus.

Facing the holy rock on the crest eastward, the worshipers now bow to the earth in prayer, for the Samaritans always face their Holy of Holies wherever they are.

The service begins with a prayer written some seven centuries ago by the priest Hassan el Suri. As it is repeated in concert, the rows of the older men and the priests kneel, or rather sit upon their heels, with hands on the knees or outstretched to heaven whenever any petition is asked. They bow their heads in unison, touching their foreheads to the ground. Some of the younger men standing behind, also with outstretched hands, join in the prayer. Throughout the service it is most interesting to watch the tiny little fellows, each beside his parent, while all follow in the repetition with as much earnestness as the grown-ups and entirely unconscious of their surroundings.

Simultaneously with the beginning of the service the sacrificial lambs have been driven into the inclosure and wander about at will, grazing upon the few tufts of green or treading upon the high priest's prayer rug till driven off.

The prayer is ended with a loud Amen! Whereupon all rise and remain perfectly erect, while in silence they repeat another prayer, called "Akid el Niyeh," a meditation which denotes the consecration of their souls to prayer. It consists of repeating the five articles of their creed—belief in God, in Moses, the Pentateuch, Mount Gerizim, and the Day of Judgment.

This and the story of creation precede all prayers. When ended a hymn is sung in praise of Yahweh, the little fellows stretching their mouths to their utmost capacity, while the older leaders, turning about from time to time, prompt and encourage the others to more

THE SPITTED SACRIFICIAL LAMBS

On oaken spits slightly longer than the depth of the ground oven, the dressed lambs are placed lengthwise, the heads hanging down. "Eat not of it raw, nor sodden at all with water; his head with his legs, and with the purtenance thereof."

fervent utterances. All these prayers, readings, and hymns are, of course, in the Samaritan Hebrew, the oldest form of that language in use.

Next, from the hand-written Pentateuch which each carries, they read in unison 21 selections, in which Abraham, Isaac, and Jacob are mentioned ("in memory of the fathers").

During the reading each time God's name is mentioned the men stroke their beards downward thrice. Likewise whenever passages are recounted enjoining them to remember their God, they bow, swinging the body forward from the hips, in token of reverence and submission.

The high priest, who has been facing the crest of Gerizim with the congregation, now turns about and repeats an antiphon, to which the leading men reply, and in conclusion a psalm is sung.

The aged high priest now mounts the fragment of an ancient column and in a low, quavering voice sings a short hymn. With his eyes upon the setting sun, he reads the first twelve verses of the twelfth chapter of Exodus, wherein are given the first commands regarding the observance of the Passover.

KILLING THE SACRIFICE

In the meantime the youths and boys have carried out the lambs and are holding them in a circle about the trench-altar, where the caldrons of water are already boiling.

Over the lambs stand three slaughterers with glistening knives of razor sharpness, for, like the Jews, only those recognized as knowing the laws regarding *kosher* and *taraf* (ritually clean and unclean meat) are allowed to do the killing. As the reading proceeds, it is so arranged that, as the passage "then shall all the convocation of the assembly of Israel slay it between the two evenings" is spoken, at the word "slay," with one deft stroke downward, each of the three slaughterers cuts one throat and jumps to the next.

In a few seconds all have been sacrificed, the white clothing of the boys holding the struggling lambs being much bespattered with blood.

Thus the passage "between the evenings" the Samaritans translate to mean between sunset and dark, the twilight hour in these lands being very short. "Thou shalt sacrifice the Passover in the evening, at the going in of the sun, at the very time thou camest forth out of Egypt."

As the slaying commences the great throngs of Samaritans and Gentiles cease to crowd about the priest who is reciting and press around the altar. All is a veritable Babel, with prayers repeated, shouting, singing, and clapping of hands.

The joy exhibited is akin to that of our children on Christmas morning or when around the blazing tree, and reminds one of the light-heartedness of the Jews when celebrating the feast of Purim, commemorating as it does the destruction of their enemy, Haman. During all this excitement some of the little Samaritan girls and boys make their way among the sacrifices, and the latter with their finger ends dot their faces with daubs of the paschal blood.

One of the young priests collects a quantity of the fresh blood in a basin and with a bunch of wild thyme vigorously stirs it; then rushes away to put a dab of it above each tent door. Upon returning he empties the remainder into the fiery ditch. "And ye shall take a bunch of hyssop, and dip it in the blood that is in the basin and strike the lintel, . . . for the Lord will pass through to smite the Egyptians; and when he seeth the blood upon the lintel the Lord will pass over (Passover) the door, and will not suffer the destroyer to come unto your houses to smite you" (Ex. 12:22, 23).

Incidentally it is of great interest that the thyme is used. Botanists have differed as to what herb the hyssop might be. Here we learn that this wild thyme has properties which keep the blood from coagulating. Besides, this custom having been handed down in unbroken succes-

"NEITHER SHALL YE BREAK A BONE THEREOF"

No forks, knives, or spoons are used at the feast and great care is observed not to break a bone. The fingers are the Samaritan's only eating utensils on this occasion.

sion, little if any room is left for doubt as to its identity with hyssop.

UNLEAVENED BREAD AND BITTER HERBS

While the lambs are giving their last life struggle, youths pass among the people bearing large trays piled high with bitter herbs, a sort of wild lettuce that grows on Gerizim, rolled in thin sheets of unleavened bread. Rolls are distributed among non-Samaritans as a token of friendship.

As the killing of the lambs commemorates the sacrifice that saved the first-born of the Hebrews from the fate of their Egyptian neighbors, so here also the eating of the bitter herbs and unleavened bread is a reminder of the bitterness of the Egyptian tyranny and the haste with which Israel left the land of the Pharaohs. "And they baked unleavened bread of the dough they brought forth out of Egypt, for it was not leavened; because they were thrust out of Egypt and could not tarry, neither had they prepared for themselves any victuals" (Ex. 12: 39).

The bread is identical with that used by the Bedouin and journeying peasants, since the baking apparatus is simple and portable, and quite likely is akin to that used during the Exodus. The loaf resembles a gigantic but very thin pancake, being pliable and not crisp like the "motsis," or unleavened bread used by the Jews at Passover.

At the sacrificial altar the older men and some of the priests, who now stand about those to whom is delegated the task of dressing the lambs, have kept up the reading of the story of the Exodus as far as to Miriam's song of triumph. Meanwhile, as soon as the lambs have become lifeless, boiling water from the caldrons is poured

SAMARITANS BAKING UNLEAVENED BREAD

The bread is made with flour quickly kneaded with water only and baked on a convex disk of sheet-iron. It is identical with that used by the Bedouin and journeying peasants. Since the baking apparatus is so simple and portable, the bread probably is much the same as that used during the Exodus. The loaf resembles a gigantic but very thin pancake.

"YE SHALL LET NOTHING OF IT REMAIN UNTIL THE MORNING"

The feast itself is of short duration. After the meat has been eaten the high priest, leaning picturesquely upon his staff, recites a short prayer. Every bit of bone remaining is now collected and taken to the altar. "And that which remaineth until the morning ye shall burn with fire." Note the two crouching figures in the foreground busily engaged in collecting and eating fragments of the roasted meat.

over them, while several boys and men crowd about in the semi-darkness and pluck off the wool instead of skinning the victims, the object being to protect the flesh while roasting in the ground oven.

THE RITUAL INSPECTION

Next the ritual inspection takes place, for as each lamb is fleeced it is suspended by its hind legs on a long pole resting on the shoulders of two of the men. The work of removing the offal, the heart, liver, and lungs is done by lantern light. Great care is taken throughout this inspection not to mutilate a bone, for the command "neither shall ye break a bone thereof" is strictly observed. Any carcass found ritually unfit is put on the burning altar and consumed with the offal. This, however, is a rare exception. The last time it happened was some five years ago, when a lamb was found minus a kidney.

Unlike the Jews, who will not eat of the hind quarters of any animal until all the sinews have been entirely removed, the Samaritans claim to know exactly the cord the angel touched while wrestling with Jacob at the ford of the Jabbok, and now a deep incision is made in the flank and it is taken out. "And Jacob was left alone; and there wrestled a man with him. And when he saw that he prevailed not against him, he touched the hollow of his thigh; and the hollow of Jacob's thigh was out of joint. . . . Therefore the children of Israel eat not of the sinew which shrank, which is upon the hollow of the thigh, unto this day" (Gen. 32: 24-32).

Deep gashes are made in the fleshy parts in order that the salt may penetrate, while the right shoulder is cut off to be roasted on a separate spit, being a priestly portion. Pieces of the head are also reserved for the priests. Only the males of the priestly family and women of the same blood, if unmarried into other families, may partake of them. "And this shall be the priest's due from the people, from them that offer a sacrifice, whether it be ox or sheep; and they shall give unto the priests the shoulder and the two cheeks."

Now an oaken spit, the length being slightly greater than the depth of the ground oven, is thrust through each dressed lamb lengthwise, the head hanging downward. To prevent the meat slipping off, a wooden pin is driven through the spit three or four spans above the lower end, and on it rests a crossboard.

As the preparation of each lamb is completed, much salt is rubbed into the flesh. "And every oblation of thy meat offering shalt thou season with salt, neither shalt thou suffer the salt of the covenant of thy God to be lacking from thy meat offering: and with all thy offerings thou shalt offer salt" (Lev. 2: 13).

THE BURNT OFFERING

This mandate is also closely observed in the matter of the burnt offering, for the viscera as collected are emptied of undigested food and then thoroughly salted, and, with the fat from the inwards and the kidneys are placed upon cloven pieces of wood laid across one end of the ditch-altar, and the fuel under it now is ignited from the fire beneath the caldrons. The burning goes on slowly till the early morning hours.

But long before these preparations have been completed the readings have come to an end, while all those at work and the onlookers shout incessantly, "We call and we affirm, there is no God but God." In fact, they aim to keep

THE SAMARITANS ASSEMBLED UPON THE SACRED ROCK

A few of the devout members of the congregation do not dare advance to the rock itself because of certain scruples regarding their ablutions. These individuals may be descried in the background kneeling like their brothers on the rock, their faces turned toward the holy spot.

this up all night, but there are numerous interruptions.

Once the service has come to an end, all those not engaged bow forward and kiss the hand of the high priest, saying in Hebrew, "Every year may you have peace." He in turn gives each his benediction and retires to his tent.

HOW THE MEAT IS COOKED

It is now only about four hours before midnight and the sides of the ground oven are glowing with heat. The white-robed figures, with much shouting and commotion, bring the spits forward, holding them in a circle about the fiery pit. With loud voices they repeat, "Hear O Israel, the Lord our God is one Lord," and passages of Scripture in which they are admonished to observe diligently the law.

Suddenly the spits are simultaneously lowered into the oven and a wickerwork lid made of sticks placed over the top, the spits protruding slightly and so held in place. Grass, sod, and mud, previously collected for the purpose, are placed over this, closely sealing the lid, so that

HANDS OUTSPREAD TO HEAVEN

"And it was so, that when Solomon had made an end of praying all this prayer and supplication unto the Lord, he rose from kneeling on his knees with his hands spread up to heaven." It was then the custom with the Hebrew nation, as still with the small remnant of the Samaritans, to spread forth the hands toward heaven. One object entirely out of harmony with the picturesqueness of this scene is the 20th century steamer chair in the center of the group of worshipers. It appealed to the Samaritans, however, as a convenient resting place for the sacred scroll in preference to the quaint but clumsy wooden stands of the synagogue.

no smoke or steam can escape, and thus extinguishing the fire; but the heat of the stones is sufficient to roast the tender mutton. "Eat not of it raw, nor sodden at all with water, but roast with fire; his head with his legs, and with the purtenance thereof" (Ex. 12: 9).

THE EVENING PRAYER

Once these duties are over the men again collect for prayer. It is now well into the night. Beginning, as usual, in silence, with their creed

and the repetition of the story of creation, Pentateuch selections pertaining to the Passover and the patriarchs are read. Between the first selections hymns are sung.

A lengthy rotation now takes place: Joshua's prayer, one that Samaritan tradition asserts he was in the habit of using; singing the song of Moses at the Red Sea, and the "Angel's Song." The main feature, however, is the clothing of the high priest or his representative with a silken cloth. The priest now presents to view one of

SAMARITAN PILGRIMS AT PRAYER IN FRONT OF THE HOLY ROCK

During the greater part of the service the high priest with staff in hand stands facing the sacred scroll, which has been placed before the Rock. He leads the congregation in reading.

the ancient Pentateuchs, one in book form, written on parchment.

It is an impressive sight when these white figures in the bright moonlight, kneeling thrice and prostrating themselves to the ground, always toward their Holy of Holies, repeat in unison, "It is a night to be much observed unto the Lord for bringing them out of the land of Egypt; this is that night of the Lord to be observed of all the children of Israel in their generations."

Thus the three Passover services are ended. The first, before the lambs are slaughtered, is called "Salat el Dabih" (Sacrificial prayers); the next, while the fleecing is taking place, "Salat el Jismeet" (Scalding prayers), and "Salat el Garub" (Sunset prayers). Under ordinary circumstances prayers are always said at even, but since the Passover service is the more important, the evening prayer is unavoidably delayed.

WHERE ARE THE WOMEN?

During the afternoon and the early evening the women have played no role in the scene. They have kept to their tents, while those unable to make their ablutions, and therefore prohibited from eating the Passover, are confined in one tent.

Like the older but now passing Jewish and native Christian custom, the Samaritan women do not strictly hide from men, but only veil when on the street and keep out of the way when strangers are present.

The present paper is written after having witnessed the Passover ceremony four times—twice before the great world conflict and twice during it. The first occasion was when the author was a youth, the second in 1914.

On both of those occasions the women were hardly seen, eating their portion of the sac-

BETROTHED

Among the Samaritans, as with most Orientals, the parents of the children arrange the matches. The betrothal often takes place when the bride and bridegroom are mere infants, while early marriages are the rule.

rifice in the tents, some of the little girls alone showing themselves. During the years of the war this phase of the scene materially changed. There were no tourists or professors, with large

SAMARITANS AT PRAYER ON THE EVE OF THE PILGRIMAGE

During the entire week following the Feast of the Passover, the Samaritans remain encamped upon Mount Gerizim. On the last day of the encampment they begin at dawn a pilgrimage to the crest of the sacred mount. Before setting forth on this pilgrimage, however, the men spread their prayer cloths and repeat the creed and the story of the creation in silence, after which, in a loud voice, they read in unison the Book of Genesis and the first quarter of the Book of Exodus, ending with the story of the Passover and the flight from Egypt.

cork hats and western clothing; no note books and pencils; no inquisitive questions to embarrass the women or to mar the ancient atmosphere of the spectacle.

Once the sacrifice had been slain, the crowds from Nablus, smaller these years than

A SAMARITAN BABY

When photographed, this child was the picture of health. Shortly after, he became ill and the mother always attributed the misfortune to the "evil eye" of the camera or of the photographer.

usual, descended and the Samaritans were left alone. In the moonlight there was no sight nor sound foreign to the surroundings to distract one's attention, and the imagination was given rein. The conception wandered back thousands of years, and one only awoke with a start to the reality of living in the twentieth century when a sudden flash of magnesium powder lit up the sky and then left all in deep darkness.

The evening prayers over, some retire to rest in their tents, some pray or read to keep awake, while not a few sit around the smoldering altar watching that every scrap is burned.

No sooner are we left alone with the Samaritans than the women begin to appear. They whose lives are so immersed in small things that they seldom leave their homes, the older women having no education at all, find great pleasure in the freedom of sitting around the sacrificial altar, conversing in their native tongue with Mrs. Whiting, and enthusiastically displaying their babies, awake or asleep, at this late hour.

OPENING THE ROASTING PIT

Thus the three to four hours between putting the lambs to roast and the time of the feast roll quickly by. Incidentally we retire to our tent and dine on roast lamb, killed and prepared by peasants of the neighboring villages in identically the same style as the paschal lambs, except that the skin is removed, for no non-Samaritan is ever allowed to partake of the sacrifice. "And the Lord said to Moses and Aaron, This is the ordinance of the Passover: There shall no stranger eat thereof."

It is because of this injunction that the Samaritans so scrupulously collect and burn any scraps cut away during the inspection, and that the burning altar is so rigorously guarded.

WAVING THE SACRED SCROLL,
ONE OF THE CEREMONIES DURING THE SAMARITAN PILGRIMAGE
TO THE HOLY ROCK, WHICH FOLLOWS THE CELEBRATION OF THE PASSOVER

The high priest, taking the sacred scroll from its resting place, holds it in his arms. Then he raises it over his head and the copper case is unfolded, so that the parchment is exposed toward the devotees, who stroke their faces and beards in reverence.

**THE SACRED SCROLL OF THE SAMARITANS
USED ON GERIZIM (REAR VIEW)**

The scroll is contained in a copper case inlaid with silver and gold,
with designs representing the temple sacrificial altar, table of shew-
bread, the golden censer, cup of manna, and other temple furnishings.

the camp is again astir. The youths with hands and hoe remove the seal from the oven, and clouds of steam pour out; so that, even with the aid of a lantern, little can be seen. It is interesting to notice the air of hurry, although time is of no consequence. The cover is now lifted with much shouting and screaming, and the same prayer said as when the lambs were placed in the oven. At once the spits are withdrawn and closely guarded while the meat is slipped off, each lamb into one of the great copper pans, the shoulders being put with the portion for the priestly family and taken to the prayer inclosure, just beyond the still burning altar.

EATING THE MEATS OF THE PASSOVER

Some of the flesh, being overdone, falls from the spits, and one of the men volunteers to rescue it. Winding bits of sacking about his hands to prevent blistering them, he is lowered into the oven. Quickly the meat is collected in a basket.

Only two men have remained near the pit, and they become so engrossed with the meat basket that the man in the pit is temporarily forgotten. The heat is more than anyone can endure longer than a few seconds, but the shouts of the unfortunate go

Even after the ceremony is at an end, the ditch and oven are filled with stones lest any remaining charred bone or fragment fall into the possession of a Gentile.

As the midnight hour approaches, the sleepers are awakened by callers and suddenly unheeded until a Gentile sends his fellows to the rescue.

The members of the six Samaritan families have now collected each around one of the lambs—men, women, children, and nursing babies. The elders and the priests arrive, each girded about his outer clothing, shod and bearing a staff or cane in imitation of the equip-

EATING THE PASSOVER

The members of the six families collect, each around one of the lambs—men, women, children, and nursing babies.

THE BIBLICAL SALUTATION: PALESTINE

Embracing one another, the head is put on the other's shoulder or neck, the latter being bent forward, and in doing so the cheek or neck is kissed, alternating from one shoulder to the other. "And Esau ran to meet him (Jacob) and embraced him, and fell upon his neck, and kissed him." The Samaritans are the tallest people in Palestine.

ment on the flight from Egypt. Now the meat is sprinkled with minced bitter herbs, and straw trays of unleavened bread are placed at hand. The high priest, in the midst, in quavering tones, says: "In the name of God I call, 'Hear O Israel, our God is one God,'" etc., while all voices join in singing an ancient Exodus hymn in which mention is made of the multitudes of

Israel that left Egypt as the issue of only seventy souls who went down into that land in the days of Joseph.

Every one now begins to eat ravenously, pulling the meat from the bones with the fingers. No forks or knives are used, and great care is observed not to break a bone. The flesh is consumed quickly, for the devout are truly hungry, having eaten little substantial food during the previous day. "And they shall eat the flesh in that night, roast with fire, and unleavened bread; and with bitter herbs they shall eat it. And thus shall ye eat it: with your loins girdled, your shoes on your feet, and your staff in your hand: and ye shall eat it in haste: it is the Lord's Passover" (Ex. 12: 8 and 11).

Those who are unable to leave their tents because of sickness have a portion sent to them, and, no matter how ill, they always partake of a little. Even the nursing babies have their lips touched with a morsel, all in literal compliance with the command that any one refraining from eating it shall be cut off from Israel.

Within a few minutes the meal is over and the high priest, leaning picturesquely upon his staff, recites a short prayer. Every bit and bone remaining is now collected and taken to the altar. Across the end where the offal has been burned the wickerwork oven cover is now thrown, and upon it all the spits are piled, together with the bones and leavings. A fire is lighted under them. Every person now washes with hot water from the kettles, pouring it over his hands from ewers, so that it also flows into the ditch-altar, lest even this infinitesimal quantity of the sacrifice should fail to be destroyed by fire. "And ye shall let nothing of it remain until the morning; and that which remaineth until the morning, ye shall burn with fire" (Ex. 12:10).

Thus the sacrifice and ceremony commemorating the Exodus are ended.

Each celebrant now goes to his tent for a few hours' sleep. Early the next morning the congregation again gathers for prayers, the day being observed as a Sabbath; the first day of the feast of unleavened bread.

As the onlooker retires to his tent or descends the path to Nablus in the hush of early morning, the scene, brightly lit by the moon, is one not to be forgotten.

From beyond the camp a great white cloud of smoke curls skyward. Now and then a red flame licks the sky or a white, ghost-like figure adds some fuel. It is a picture which cannot be reproduced with the camera; only to the mind's eye can it be painted. The wood-cuts and steel-engravings found in our old family Bibles, where the Israelitish camps are shown with the pillar of cloud and fire, come nearest the present reality, but are lacking in color and atmosphere.

As we turn for one last glance at the moonlit camp and the redder glow of the flame with the pillar of smoke, we cannot but realize that here we have seen the eating and burning of the last Hebrew blood sacrifice, and there comes the thought that it may never be seen again, for the Samaritans are a dying people.

FURTHER READING

An excellent survey of the Holy Land between 1914 and 1920 is Ronald Sanders, *The High Walls of Jerusalem: A History of the Balfour Declaration and the Birth of the British Mandate for Palestine* (1983). See also Karen Armstrong, *Jerusalem* (1996). This volume contains an excellent ten-page bibliography. Joe H. Kirchberger, *The First World War* (1992) and S.L.A. Marshall, *World War I* (1964) cover Palestine during the war. *At the Wall* (1998) by the celebrated photographer Ron Agam offers a unique history of Jerusalem through the eyes of his camera.

INDEX

CONTRIBUTORS

General Editor FRED L. ISRAEL is an award-winning historian. He received the Scribe's Award from the American Bar Association for his work on the Chelsea House series *The Justices of the United States Supreme Court*. A specialist in American history, he was general editor for Chelsea's *1897 Sears Roebuck Catalog*. Dr. Israel has also worked in association with Arthur M. Schlesinger, jr. on many projects, including *The History of the U.S. Presidential Elections* and *The History of U.S. Political Parties*. He is senior consulting editor on the Chelsea House series *Looking into the Past: People, Places, and Customs*, which examines past traditions, customs, and cultures of various nations.

Senior Consulting Editor ARTHUR M. SCHLESINGER, JR. is the preeminent American historian of our time. He won the Pulitzer Prize for his book *The Age of Jackson* (1945), and again for *A Thousand Days* (1965). This chronicle of the Kennedy Administration also won a National Book Award. He has written many other books, including a multi-volume series, *The Age of Roosevelt*. Professor Schlesinger is the Albert Schweitzer Professor of the Humanities at the City University of New York, and has been involved in several other Chelsea House projects, including the *American Statesmen* series of biographies on the most prominent figures of early American history.